WILLIAMS·SONOMA

eat well

AUTHOR
Charity Ferreira

GENERAL EDITOR
Chuck Williams

PHOTOGRAPHER
Kana Okada

Oxmoor House.

contents

about this book

Charity Ferreira cooks the way I love to eat. A chef by training, she is devoted to enjoying good food. But she also knows how to bring a healthful sense of balance to the table. She understands how people like to think about their meals: not in terms of nutrients and kilojoules, but in terms of what they're in the mood to eat. So whether you have a hankering for Asian tonight, a big salad, or a substantial grilled meat dish, with her book you can satisfy your craving with a delicious meal that also happens to be good for you, featuring health-enhancing ingredients or employing a lighter cooking technique.

A casual reader looking for great meals will find plenty to love about *Eat Well*, with its mouthwatering variety of recipes and vibrant photographs. For diners particularly focused on good health, nutritional labels on each recipe and a complete analysis in the back of the book smooth the path to eating right. *Eat Well* is a new breed of healthy cookbook that offers recipes so tempting we can all see it's no punishment to do your body good.

Chuck Williams

eating healthy & well

Eating well: It means being well fed, well nourished, and well satisfied. Food sustains our bodies, but as we've long known, it also satisfies another part of us. Eating well nourishes our hearts and spirits with varied, balanced, wholesome food that is pleasurable to make, beautiful to look at, and, above all, delicious to eat.

life in balance

It seems that the more advances science makes in discovering what is good for us, the more basic the overall message remains. In an age of supersized junk food on the one hand and odd, often contradictory bits of dietary information taken out of context on the other, the truth is that there's no magical shortcut to eating well. Whole foods in their natural state—grains, vegetables and fruits, sustainably raised meats, fresh seafood—are the foods that are best for our bodies, and it's no accident that they are also the foods that taste best when prepared simply.

Whether cooking is a passionate hobby of yours, or whether you are just looking for a few simple, healthy meals to make every week to feed your family, in this book you'll find delightfully easy ways to prepare some of the healthiest, most naturally delicious foods you can eat. As you browse through this book, you might be surprised to find that many of these healthy choices are foods that you already love.

start and end the day right

The day, and our book, begins and ends with two of the most important meals: breakfast and dessert. Breakfast kick-starts your metabolism first thing in the morning, refueling your body after its long fast. Many studies have extolled the virtues of eating breakfast and have suggested that a good breakfast leads to better concentration at work or school and a decrease in the tendency to overeat later in the day. And far from being an "extra" or forbidden course, dessert is a chance to end the day with a taste of something wholesome and sweet. Eating well means enjoying all foods in moderation, and lingering over a sweet dessert with family and friends after a busy day or long week is an important part of eating well.

peak-of-season produce

Eating well means eating fresh food. Fruits and vegetables are welcome at every meal, and make the best snacks in between. The Big Salads and Farmers' Market Fresh chapters offer multiple delicious opportunities to eat vegetables and fruits in every color of the rainbow. If you make fresh produce a cornerstone of your diet, you will reap the benefits with a noticeable surge in energy and vitality. Turn to these chapters to discover some new favorite dishes to help you take advantage of the natural goodness

of fresh produce, from winter broccoli to spring asparagus to summer zucchini and autumn squash.

powerful protein

Lean animal protein is the star of the Lean & Mean and Seafood for Dinner chapters. The role that protein plays in a healthy diet has commanded no shortage of attention and debate in recent years due to the popularity of high-protein diets. While a surfeit of protein is known to be unhealthy and a strain on the body, one benefit of lean protein is that it is uniquely satisfying and filling, so eating it at meals can help curb snacking or grazing and keep your overall diet moderate and well balanced. But animal protein isn't the only kind; whole grains and legumes offer excellent alternative proteins without saturated fat. Turn to the Meatless Meals chapter for a great selection of dishes.

world's healthiest cuisines

A tour of the world's healthiest cuisines awaits you in the Mediterranean Tonight, Asian Tonight, and California Cuisine Tonight chapters. These regions of the world are noted for the healthfulness of their cuisines and their emphasis on fresh, wholesome ingredients and simple, delicious preparations. Whatever kind of food you're in the mood for on any particular night, you'll find great choices in these chapters.

Eating well means that every bite we take should be both nourishing and delicious. Every meal or snack we choose or prepare throughout the day is an opportunity to nurture our bodies and improve our well-being. This book is divided into chapters that make the most of the day's plentiful opportunities for eating well.

how to use this book

Balanced eating is an essential part of balanced living. Eating well keeps your body healthy and helps it perform at its best. A well-rounded diet has benefits that go beyond supplying our bodies with the necessary nutrients. The recipes in this book prove that healthful food can be a joy to prepare, serve, and eat.

wholesome variety

Along with offering simple, wholesome recipes using nutritious ingredients, this cookbook has several features to help make it convenient to eat a varied, healthful diet every day.

spotlight on superfoods

While variety is the key to healthy eating, some foods pack a superior nutritional punch. These foods should always find a place on your menu and your shopping list. You'll find features throughout this book on fourteen of the most common "superfoods." Read about why to include them in your diet, then enjoy simple ways of preparing them.

what's for dinner?

Life's daily demands can make it easy to fall into a food rut, especially during the work week. To keep some of the most versatile, wholesome ingredients from getting boring, certain chapters feature "4 Ways" to cook a healthy, easily purchased staple, such as chicken breasts, fish fillets, or canned beans. Turn to these sections when you need a quick, delicious weeknight supper.

the pleasure of real food

Hearty, lightly dressed salads. Bright, fresh vegetables cooked just until tender yet crisp. Savory, earthy whole grains. Simply grilled meats and seafood. Eating a balanced, moderate, wholesome diet does not need to feel like penance. We hope you'll discover some new favorite dishes in this book that will help you relish and enjoy the natural goodness of fresh, whole foods.

healthy recipe labels

When you're browsing through this cookbook in search of a recipe, check the bottom line: Each is labeled so you can identify two key nutritional properties at a glance, helping to keep your menu and your body well balanced.

source of vitamins These are recipes that are especially high in one or more of the thirteen vitamins essential for maintaining good health. Whether it's A, C, D, E, K, or any of the B vitamins, all of the vitamins your body needs can come from a balanced diet rather than in a pill.

source of minerals Minerals such as calcium, magnesium, potassium, zinc, and iron support the body's biochemical systems. Recipes with this label are high in one or more essential minerals.

source of antioxidants The darling of current nutritional research, compounds known as antioxidants have been shown to protect against, and even repair, cellular damage, and have been linked to heart health and cancer prevention. To help you incorporate a healthy amount of antioxidants into your diet each day, look for the recipes with this label.

source of good fats A healthy diet includes fat. Specifically, poly- and monounsaturated fats have been linked

to heart health. And some vitamins (such as A, D, E, and K) and minerals are fat soluble, which means that fat aids their absorption by the body. The American Heart Association recommends limiting your intake of saturated fat, which is linked to increased blood cholesterol. Recipes high in heart-healthy omega-3 fats are specifically labeled as well.

source of lean protein Proteins are the body's building blocks, important for the growth and replacement of cells. The best sources of protein are lean beef, poultry, fish, eggs, dairy products, nuts, seeds, and legumes. Recipes featuring these protein-rich ingredients are noted.

source of fiber Fiber-rich diets have been linked with both digestive and cardiovascular health. This label will help you identify recipes with a good portion of fiber. Certain forms of fiber—such as the kind found in oat bran—are known to lower cholesterol levels, so they get a "cholesterol-buster" label.

calcium-rich A mineral lacking in many people's diets, calcium is vital to maintaining bone health, and is important for other biochemical functions as well. Women in particular are advised to get all the calcium they need for bone health later in life—and calcium has the welcome side benefit of helping you to maintain a trim figure.

iron-rich Iron is a mineral that helps the body transport and use oxygen. It plays a role in immune function, cognitive development, temperature regulation, and energy metabolism. Many women consume less iron than they need.

whole grain Whole grains offer many advantages over their refined and polished counterparts, most notably their association with a reduced risk of cardiovascular disease and stroke.

live culture When buying yogurt, look for a label on the package indicating that it contains live cultures. These colonies of "good" bacteria, which are used to thicken milk into yogurt, have many beneficial effects on the body, ranging from keeping the digestive tract healthy to increasing immunity and preventing disease.

beverage bar

The chapters that follow offer delicious ways to eat well throughout the day, but you'll need a glass of something fresh and flavorful to raise with your meals! Here is a quintet of antioxidant-rich fruit- and tea-based beverages to satisfy your thirst.

1 *green tea cooler*

green tea, 2 2/3 cups brewed and cooled

pineapple juice, 1 1/3 cups

honey, 1/4 cup

lime juice, 2 Tbsp

ice cubes, for serving

fresh pineapple chunks, for garnish

Stir all ingredients except ice cubes and garnish together in a pitcher until honey is dissolved. Serve in tall chilled glasses over ice, garnished with fresh pineapple.

4 SERVINGS

2 *iced darjeeling tea*

blackberries, 3/4 cup

fresh mint leaves, 8–12

sugar, 8 tsp

ice cubes, 2–4 cups

Darjeeling tea, 4 cups brewed and cooled

Put 4–5 blackberries, 2–3 mint leaves, and 2 tsp sugar in the bottom of each of 4 tall glasses. Use a wooden spoon to coarsely crush berries and mint. Fill each glass halfway with ice cubes and add 1 cup tea. Stir gently and serve at once.

4 SERVINGS

3 *pomegranate pink lemonade*

pomegranate juice, 1 1/2 cups

lemon juice, 1/2 cup

sugar, 1/4 cup

ice cubes, for serving

lemon twists, for serving

Stir 2 cups water, juices, and sugar together in a pitcher until sugar is dissolved. Serve in chilled glasses over ice, garnished with a lemon twist.

4 SERVINGS

4 *cantaloupe agua fresca*

ripe cantaloupe, 1 1/2 lb

sugar, 1/4 cup

lime juice, 3 Tbsp

ice cubes, for serving

Peel and seed cantaloupe and cut into 1-inch pieces. In a blender, purée cantaloupe, sugar, and 1/2 cup water until very smooth. Pour into a pitcher and whisk in 3 1/2 cups water and lime juice. Serve in chilled glasses over ice.

4 SERVINGS

5 *ginger limeade*

sugar, 1 cup

fresh ginger, 1/2 cup thinly sliced

ice cubes, 2–4 cups

lime juice, 10 Tbsp

club soda or sparkling water, 4 cups

lime slices, for garnish (optional)

In a small saucepan, stir sugar, 1 cup water, and ginger over low heat until sugar is dissolved. Bring mixture to a simmer and cook for 3 minutes. Remove from heat and let stand for 1 hour. Pour syrup through a fine-mesh strainer, pressing on ginger with a flexible spatula to extract as much liquid as possible. Discard ginger.

Fill 4 tall glasses half full with ice cubes. Add 2 1/2 Tbsp lime juice and 3 Tbsp ginger syrup to each glass and stir gently. Pour 1 cup club soda into each glass. Garnish with a slice or two of lime, if desired. Stir gently.

4 SERVINGS

breakfast

Mom was right when she told you that breakfast was the most important meal of the day. It's also the meal we're most likely to skip in our rush to get out the door in the morning. But it's worth sparing a little time to fuel up: Eating a hearty, healthy breakfast can make a big difference to your well-being all day long. Whether you crave sweet or savory flavors first thing in the morning, you'll find plenty of dishes in this chapter to give you a head start on your protein, calcium, and fiber for the day. Whether you choose a whole-grain dish like Irish Porridge with Strawberries & Cream or Maple-Almond Granola, a nutritious egg dish like Shirred Eggs with Spinach & Paprika or Root-Vegetable Hash Topped with Poached Eggs, a healthier twist on a traditional favorite, such as Buckwheat Pancakes Studded with Blueberries, or a sweet and satisfying novelty like Breakfast Panini with Almond Butter & Plum Preserves, you'll find plenty here to start your day off well.

This crunchy granola, lightly sweetened with honey and flavorful grade-B maple syrup, is very versatile; you can stir in almost any type of fresh or dried fruit (such as currants or cranberries) once the granola is cool. Enjoy it out of hand as a snack, sprinkle over yogurt, or serve in a bowl with milk.

maple-almond granola
with seasonal fruit

canola oil, ¼ cup

grade B maple syrup, ½ cup

honey, ¼ cup

salt, ¼ tsp

rolled oats, 4 cups

coarsely chopped almonds, 1 cup

fresh or dried fruit, for serving

Preheat oven to 325°F. Lightly oil a 12-by-15-inch baking pan.

In a large bowl, whisk together oil, syrup, honey, and salt. Stir in oats and almonds, mixing to coat them completely. Spread evenly in prepared pan and bake, stirring every 10 minutes, until golden brown, 30–35 minutes. Cool completely. Store granola in an airtight container at room temperature for up to 2 weeks. Top with fruit to serve.

MAKES 10 SERVINGS • SOURCE OF FIBER • CHOLESTEROL-BUSTER

This method for quick plum preserves is an easy way to make a small amount of jam without having to use canning jars or pectin. Be sure to choose organic plums and leave the skins on; not only do the skins add antioxidants, color, and flavor, but they also help to thicken the preserves.

breakfast panini
with almond butter & plum preserves

Halve, pit, and coarsely chop plums. In a saucepan, stir plums and sugar over low heat until plums have released their juices and sugar is dissolved, 5–8 minutes. Bring to a simmer and cook, uncovered, until mixture thickens and plums have a jamlike consistency, 25–30 minutes. Stir in lemon juice. Cool to room temperature, then cover and refrigerate for up to 2 weeks.

Preheat a nonstick panini maker according to the manufacturer's directions. Spread 1–2 Tbsp almond butter on each of 2 slices of bread. Spoon about 2 Tbsp ricotta over almond butter. Spread about 1 Tbsp of the plum preserves on each of the remaining 2 slices of bread. Assemble sandwiches and toast in panini maker until crisp and golden, 3–5 minutes. (If you have a panini maker that allows you to exert pressure to flatten the sandwich, don't compress too much, or you will lose some delicious filling.)

2 SANDWICHES • SOURCE OF OMEGA-3S • SOURCE OF VITAMINS

red-skinned plums, 1½ lb

sugar, 1 cup

lemon juice, 1 Tbsp

almond butter, 2–4 Tbsp

country-style bread, 4 slices (½ inch thick)

part-skim ricotta cheese, 4 Tbsp

oats

Oats have long been touted for their health benefits. Study after study has shown the fiber in oats to have positive effects on cholesterol levels. But the benefits of adding oats to your diet don't end there. In addition to fiber, oats also contain essential vitamins and minerals, protein, and heart-healthy antioxidants. Regular consumption of oatmeal has also been linked with the prevention of type 2 diabetes. In short, a bowl of oats is one of the best ways you can start your day.

Oats are available in several forms. Steel-cut oats are hulled and cut into small, nubby particles. Sometimes called Irish oatmeal or Scotch oats, they have a nutty flavor and chewy texture, and cook in 30 to 45 minutes. Rolled oats are hulled, steamed grains that have been rolled into flakes that take between 5 and 15 minutes on the stove top. Instant oatmeal, because it has been further processed, lacks much of the fiber and whole-grain benefits of other forms of oats, and sometimes contains a surprising amount of sugar.

Because of their relatively high fat content, oats are prone to rancidity if stored too long. Keep them in a cool, dry place for up to 2 months.

irish porridge
with strawberries & cream

In a medium saucepan over medium-high heat, combine 4 cups water, oats, and ⅛ tsp salt and bring to a simmer. Reduce heat to maintain a gentle simmer, cover, and cook, stirring occasionally, until oats are tender and creamy, about 30 minutes.

Spoon porridge into 4 bowls and top each bowl with ¼ cup strawberries, 1 Tbsp cream, and 2 tsp sugar. Serve at once.

4 SERVINGS • CHOLESTEROL-BUSTER • SOURCE OF VITAMINS

steel-cut oats, 1 cup

salt

strawberries, 1 cup coarsely chopped

heavy cream, 4 Tbsp

light brown or turbinado sugar, 8 tsp

oatmeal
with pumpkin & cinnamon

In a medium saucepan, bring 3½ cups water to a boil. Stir in oats, cinnamon, and a pinch of salt. Reduce heat to medium-low. Simmer, stirring occasionally, until oats are tender and liquid is absorbed, 4–5 minutes or according to package directions. Stir in pumpkin and cook until heated through, 1 minute longer. Stir in raisins and brown sugar. Spoon into bowls and serve at once, with milk if you like.

4 SERVINGS • CHOLESTEROL-BUSTER • SOURCE OF VITAMINS

old-fashioned (not quick-cooking) rolled oats, 2 cups

ground cinnamon, ½ tsp

salt

canned pumpkin purée, ½ cup

golden raisins, ¼ cup

brown sugar, ¼ cup firmly packed

milk, for serving (optional)

Eggs baked in individual ramekins are an easy, cheery breakfast. You can vary the doneness of the eggs by adjusting the baking time; begin checking them after 10 minutes for soft-set eggs with runny yolks. Thick-sliced sourdough toast makes a perfect accompaniment to round out this breakfast.

shirred eggs
with spinach & paprika

olive oil spray

baby spinach leaves, 4 oz
coarsely chopped (1 1/3 cups)

extra-large eggs, 4

heavy cream, 2 Tbsp

salt and freshly ground pepper

paprika, for sprinkling

Preheat oven to 375°F. Coat insides of four 6-oz ramekins generously with olive oil spray. Put about 1/3 cup spinach in each ramekin and crack an egg into each ramekin over the spinach. Drizzle 1/2 Tbsp cream over each egg and sprinkle with salt, pepper, and paprika.

Bake until egg whites are firm and yolks are as runny or firm as desired, 10–14 minutes. Serve at once.

4 SERVINGS • SOURCE OF VITAMINS • CALCIUM-RICH

The oats in these scones gives them extra fiber as well as a pleasantly flaky, crumbly texture. For best results, look for old-fashioned rolled oats, which have a sturdy texture and more fiber than more processed instant oats. Bake a batch of these hearty scones on the weekend and keep them in the freezer to rewarm on busy weekday mornings.

oatmeal scones
with cherries, walnuts & chocolate chunks

Preheat oven to 350°F. Lightly butter a baking sheet or line it with parchment paper.

In a bowl, stir together flour, oats, sugar, baking powder, baking soda, and salt. Using a pastry blender or 2 knives, cut in butter until mixture resembles coarse crumbs.

In a small bowl, whisk together buttermilk and egg. Add to flour mixture along with cherries, walnuts, and chocolate. Stir with a fork just until evenly moistened (dough will still look crumbly).

Scrape dough onto a floured surface and, with lightly floured hands, work together into a ball. Divide into 8 equal pieces and gently pat each piece into a 2 1/2-inch round about 1 1/2 inches thick. Place rounds 2 inches apart on prepared baking sheet.

Bake scones until tops are browned, 25–30 minutes. Cool for about 10 minutes on baking sheet before serving.

8 SCONES • CHOLESTEROL-BUSTER • SOURCE OF OMEGA-3S

all-purpose flour, 2 cups
old-fashioned rolled oats, 1 cup
sugar, 1/4 cup
baking powder, 1 Tbsp
baking soda, 2 tsp
salt, 1/2 tsp
cold unsalted butter, 6 Tbsp, cut into pieces
buttermilk, 3/4 cup
large egg, 1
dried tart cherries, 1/2 cup
walnuts, 1/2 cup coarsely chopped
dark chocolate chunks, 1/2 cup

Crisp on the outside, tender on the inside, these waffles make a delicious whole-grain breakfast. Because they're not too sweet, the waffles alone also make a nice base for a fried egg sandwich, or even a side dish to accompany roast chicken. Keep the waffles warm in a low oven as you make them.

multigrain ricotta waffles
with strawberries & yogurt

all-purpose flour, 1 cup

whole-wheat flour, ½ cup

stone-ground cornmeal, ½ cup

sugar, 1 Tbsp

baking powder, 2 tsp

salt, ½ tsp

milk, 1½ cups

part-skim ricotta cheese, ½ cup

large eggs, 2

canola oil, 3 Tbsp

plain yogurt, for serving

sliced strawberries, for serving

In a large bowl, stir together flours, cornmeal, sugar, baking powder, and salt. In another bowl, whisk together milk, ricotta, eggs, and oil. Stir milk mixture into flour mixture just until smooth.

Coat a waffle iron lightly with oil, wiping off any excess with a paper towel. Preheat to medium. Spoon about ½ cup batter onto hot waffle iron, spreading it out to the edges. Cook until golden brown, 3–5 minutes. Repeat with remaining batter.

Serve waffles with a dollop of yogurt on top, scattered with sliced strawberries.

6 WAFFLES, 4–6 SERVINGS • WHOLE GRAIN • LIVE CULTURE

When buying yogurt, choose one that contains "live and active cultures." The beneficial bacteria in this type of yogurt are thought to boost the immune system, increase the absorption of nutrients, and keep the intestinal tract healthy.

4 WAYS WITH yogurt

strawberry-banana smoothie

ripe banana, 1

fresh orange juice, ½ cup

frozen strawberries or mixed berries, ½ cup

vanilla low-fat or nonfat yogurt, 1 cup

Peel and break banana into chunks.

In a blender or food processor, combine banana, orange juice, and strawberries. Process until mixture is smooth, 30–45 seconds.

Add yogurt and process until thoroughly blended, about 20 seconds longer.

Pour smoothie into 2 tall glasses and serve at once.

2 SERVINGS • LIVE CULTURE • CALCIUM-RICH

carrot-pineapple smoothie

frozen pineapple chunks, 2 cups

carrot juice, ½ cup

plain low-fat or nonfat yogurt, 1 cup

In a blender or food processor, combine pineapple and carrot juice. Process until mixture is smooth, 30–45 seconds.

Add yogurt and process until thoroughly blended, about 20 seconds longer.

Pour smoothie into 2 tall glasses and serve at once.

2 SERVINGS • LIVE CULTURE • SOURCE OF ANTIOXIDANTS

In addition, the yogurt in these smoothies contains a good helping of calcium, which helps maintain a trim waistline. So enjoy a quick and nourishing smoothie every morning, using any combination of fruit and other flavorings that suits you.

blueberry-pomegranate smoothie

Peel and break banana into chunks.

In a blender or food processor, combine banana, pomegranate juice, blueberries, and honey. Process until mixture is smooth, 30–45 seconds.

Add yogurt and process until thoroughly blended, about 20 seconds longer.

Pour smoothie into 2 tall glasses and serve at once.

2 SERVINGS • SOURCE OF ANTIOXIDANTS • LIVE CULTURE

ripe banana, 1

pomegranate juice, ½ cup

frozen blueberries, ½ cup

honey, 1 Tbsp

plain low-fat or nonfat yogurt, 1 cup

chocolate–peanut butter smoothie

Peel and break banana into chunks.

In a blender or food processor, combine banana, milk, peanut butter, and cocoa. Process until mixture is smooth, 30–45 seconds.

Add yogurt and process until mixture is thoroughly blended, about 20 seconds longer.

Pour smoothie into 2 tall glasses and serve at once.

2 SERVINGS • SOURCE OF GOOD FATS • LIVE CULTURE

ripe banana, 1

milk, ½ cup

creamy peanut butter, 1½ Tbsp

unsweetened cocoa powder, 1½ Tbsp

vanilla low-fat or nonfat yogurt, 1 cup

This hearty cold-weather breakfast dish of nutritious and earthy root vegetables topped with eggs is especially pretty when made with a combination of red and golden beets. Cut the potatoes last so they don't have time to discolor, and leave the skins on for a rustic look.

root-vegetable hash
topped with poached eggs

Preheat the oven to 400°F. Trim stems and tails from beets and peel them. Cut into ½-inch dice. Cut sweet potatoes and Yukon golds into ½-inch dice. Peel and chop onion.

Pour oil into a large roasting pan. Add vegetables, spreading them in a single layer, and sprinkle with garlic, ½ tsp salt, and ¼ tsp pepper. Roast, stirring every 15 minutes to scrape up any browned bits, until vegetables are tender, 45–50 minutes. Stir in parsley.

Bring a large, deep frying pan of lightly salted water to a boil. Reduce heat to a simmer. Crack eggs, 1 at a time, into a measuring cup, then gently slide each egg into water. Cook until eggs are softly set, about 3 minutes.

Divide vegetable hash among 4 plates and top each portion with a poached egg. Season eggs with salt and pepper and serve at once.

4 SERVINGS • SOURCE OF VITAMINS • SOURCE OF FIBER

red or yellow beets,
or a combination, 1 lb

sweet potatoes, ½ lb, peeled

Yukon gold or white boiling
potatoes, 1½ lb

yellow onion, 1

olive oil, 3 Tbsp

garlic, 3 cloves, minced

salt and freshly ground pepper

fresh parsley leaves, 3 Tbsp
chopped

large eggs, 4

Buckwheat flour gives these tender pancakes a slightly nutty flavor and dusky color. The key to making perfect pancakes lies in adjusting the heat to maintain the right cooking temperature. The batter should sizzle as it hits the pan, and the bottom of the pancake should be golden brown by the time bubbles form on the surface.

buckwheat pancakes
studded with blueberries

all-purpose flour, 1¼ cups

buckwheat flour, ¾ cup

baking powder, 1½ tsp

baking soda, 1½ tsp

salt, ¼ tsp

large eggs, 2

buttermilk, 2½ cups

canola oil, 2 Tbsp

fresh blueberries, 1 cup

warm maple syrup, for serving

In a large bowl, stir together all-purpose and buckwheat flours, baking powder, baking soda, and salt. In a small bowl, whisk together eggs, buttermilk, and oil until well blended. Stir egg mixture into flour mixture just until blended, then gently fold in blueberries.

Preheat oven to 200°F. Heat a 12-inch nonstick frying pan or a nonstick griddle over medium heat. Coat pan lightly with oil and carefully wipe out with a paper towel. Spoon batter into the pan in ⅓-cup portions and cook until pancakes are browned on the bottom and bubbles form on the surface, about 2 minutes. Flip pancakes and cook until second sides are browned, 1½–2 minutes longer. Keep pancakes warm in the oven while you cook remaining batter. Serve warm with maple syrup.

16–18 PANCAKES, 4–6 SERVINGS • WHOLE GRAIN

Greek yogurt is strained, making it thicker than other types of yogurt. Even when made from low-fat milk, it has a lush, silky texture and a fresh, tart flavor. Plain regular yogurt will also work well, or you can thicken yogurt yourself by refrigerating it overnight in a sieve lined with cheesecloth set over a bowl.

yogurt parfaits
with fresh fruit & honey

Preheat oven to 350°F. Spread almonds on a baking sheet and toast until fragrant and just turning golden, about 3 minutes. Remove to a plate to stop the cooking, and cool.

Spoon 1/3 cup yogurt into bottom of a large goblet or parfait glass. Spoon about 1/2 cup of fruit over yogurt. Sprinkle with 1/2 Tbsp almonds and drizzle with about 1/2 tsp honey. Repeat layers, ending with honey. Repeat to assemble 3 more parfaits. Serve at once, or refrigerate for up to 2 hours.

4 SERVINGS • LIVE CULTURE • SOURCE OF FIBER

sliced almonds, 4 Tbsp

Greek-style plain yogurt, 2 2/3 cups

fresh fruit such as plums, peaches, nectarines, or figs, 4 cups coarsely chopped

honey, 4 tsp

big salads

Fresh and colorful, a well-made salad offers bright flavors and a contrast of textures. Salads let busy cooks transform fruits, vegetables, whole grains, and protein into a proper meal without much elaborate preparation. There's almost no limit to the foods that can be tossed with flavorful vinegars and good olive oil to make a delicious, nutritious salad. A light but satisfying supper can be made of most salads in this chapter, like Watermelon & Feta Salad with Grilled Shrimp. Others, like the Roasted Sweet Potato Salad with Pecans & Green Onion, will do double duty as side dishes. Look for fresh new takes on old favorites here, like the Warm Spinach Salad with Delicata Squash & Ricotta Salata or the Chopped Cucumber Salad with Pomegranate, Feta & Mint. Perfect for warm weather, most of the salads in this chapter are served cool or at room temperature, which means that neither cooking nor eating them will slow you down.

This colorful roasted root vegetable salad is delicious alongside the Skirt Steak Salad with Oranges & Arugula on page 123. Use any variety of sweet potato you like, including the ones sometimes labeled "garnet yams," which have a bright orange color and moist, sweet flesh.

roasted sweet potato salad
with pecans & green onion

sweet potatoes, 3 lb

olive oil, 2 Tbsp

salt and freshly ground pepper

lime juice, ⅓ cup

maple syrup, 3 Tbsp

toasted pecans, ½ cup

green onions, ½ cup minced

fresh cilantro leaves, ¼ cup chopped

Preheat oven to 400°F. Peel sweet potatoes and cut into 1-inch chunks. Put in a large baking pan, drizzle with 1½ Tbsp oil, sprinkle with ½ tsp salt, and mix to coat. Spread potatoes in a single layer and bake, stirring occasionally, until tender when pierced, 25–30 minutes.

Meanwhile, in a large bowl, mix lime juice, maple syrup, and remaining ½ Tbsp oil. Add hot roasted sweet potatoes to lime juice mixture, along with pecans, green onions, and cilantro. Mix well and season to taste with pepper and additional salt. Serve at once, or cool to room temperature and mix again before serving.

4–6 SERVINGS • SOURCE OF ANTIOXIDANTS • SOURCE OF FIBER

This salad makes a stylish lunch dish or a light supper, pairing nicely with a heart-healthy light-bodied red wine such as a pinot noir or Chianti. Oranges, scallops, and even onions are at their best in the wintertime, and these lively flavors will help brighten up a gloomy afternoon or evening.

seared scallops
with orange & red onion salad

Place onion slices in a colander and rinse well under cold running water. Put in a small bowl and stir in rice vinegar. Set aside.

Zest 1 orange to yield 1 tsp, and reserve. Cut ends off all oranges, then cut away peel and pith, following curve of orange. Discard peel. Slice oranges in half lengthwise, then slice crosswise into thin half-rounds. In a bowl, combine orange slices with olives, reserved zest, and 1 Tbsp olive oil.

Season scallops lightly with salt and pepper. Heat remaining 1 Tbsp oil in a large nonstick frying pan over medium-high heat. Add scallops and cook, turning once, until browned on both sides and opaque in center, 4–5 minutes total. Take care not to overcook scallops, as they go quickly from perfectly tender to overcooked and tough.

Add onion (including vinegar), mint, a pinch of salt, and a few grindings of pepper to orange mixture and mix gently. Divide orange salad among 4 dinner plates and top with warm scallops. Serve at once.

4 SERVINGS • SOURCE OF OMEGA-3S • CHOLESTEROL-BUSTER

red onion, ½, thinly sliced
rice vinegar, 1½ Tbsp
oranges, 3
mild green olives, ½ cup pitted
extra-virgin olive oil, 2 Tbsp
sea scallops, 1½–2 inches in diameter, 1 lb
salt and freshly ground pepper
fresh mint leaves, 2 Tbsp coarsely chopped

Delicata squash, which has sweet, pale-orange flesh, is a good source of vitamins A and C, potassium, and iron. When roasted, the pretty scalloped peel of this winter squash becomes tender enough to eat. If you can't find Delicata, use cubes of cooked butternut squash or sweet potato.

warm spinach salad
with delicata squash & ricotta salata

Delicata squash, 1½ lb

olive oil, 4 Tbsp

salt and freshly ground pepper

sherry or red wine vinegar, 3 Tbsp

baby spinach leaves, 8 oz

ricotta salata or feta cheese, 4 oz, crumbled

toasted sliced almonds, ½ cup

Preheat oven to 400°F. Rinse and dry squash. Halve squash lengthwise and remove seeds, then cut crosswise into half moons ½ inch thick. In a 12-by-17-inch baking pan, toss squash with 1 Tbsp olive oil, ¼ tsp salt, and a few grindings of pepper. Bake until squash is tender, about 20 minutes.

In a large bowl, mix vinegar and ¼ tsp salt. Add squash, spinach, cheese, and almonds. Heat remaining 3 Tbsp oil in a small frying pan over medium-high heat. Carefully pour over salad (oil may splatter) and toss to coat and wilt spinach evenly. Serve at once.

4 STARTER SERVINGS • CALCIUM-RICH • SOURCE OF ANTIOXIDANTS

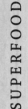

avocados

Avocados seem like an indulgent treat: They have a buttery texture, a mild and delicious flavor, and they mash beautifully into creamy guacamole. It's true that avocados are high in calories and fat, but it would be a mistake to avoid them for this reason.

These pebbly-skinned fruits that range from bright green to purplish black are loaded with nutrients that we all should be getting more of, including heart-healthy monounsaturated fats, fiber, and folate. They're also high in potassium, vitamin K, and the carotenoid lutein.

If you plan to eat them right away, choose avocados that yield to gentle pressure. If you're buying them for later in the week, chose slightly underripe avocados; they will ripen at room temperature in a few days. To remove the pit, cut the avocado in half lengthwise and rotate the halves to separate. Gently scoop out the pit with a spoon. Run a spoon gently between the flesh and the peel and lift out the flesh. Slice or dice the buttery fruit for salsas or sandwiches, or eat them as they are, with a squeeze of lime juice and a pinch of salt.

black beans & avocado
with shrimp

Put onion in a fine-mesh strainer and rinse under cold running water. Drain well. Put black beans in a colander, rinse under cold water, and drain.

Stir together onion, beans, lime juice, olive oil, jalapeño, oregano, cumin, and 1/2 tsp salt. At this point, salad can be refrigerated for up to 1 day.

Just before serving, halve and pit avocados. Scoop flesh from peel and cut into 1-inch chunks. Gently fold avocado, shrimp, and cilantro into salad and season to taste with additional salt if desired.

4–6 SERVINGS • SOURCE OF GOOD FATS • SOURCE OF LEAN PROTEIN

red onion, 1/2 cup finely chopped

black beans, 2 cans (14 1/2 oz each)

lime juice, 1/4 cup

olive oil, 1 1/2 Tbsp

jalapeño, 1, seeded and minced

dried Mexican oregano, 3/4 tsp crumbled

ground cumin, 3/4 tsp

salt

ripe avocados, 2

cooked shelled medium shrimp, 1 lb

cilantro leaves, 1/2 cup chopped

avocado & crab salad
with orange vinaigrette

In a small bowl, whisk together vinegar, orange juice, miso, tahini, and pepper flakes to make a smooth and creamy dressing.

Halve and pit avocados. Slice flesh lengthwise and scoop from peel. Core and seed bell pepper and thinly slice. Divide avocado slices and bell pepper evenly and arrange on plates. Top with crab. Spoon dressing evenly over salads and serve at once.

2 MAIN OR 4 STARTER SERVINGS • SOURCE OF GOOD FATS

rice vinegar, 3 Tbsp

fresh orange juice, 2 Tbsp

white miso, 2 tsp

tahini, 1 1/2 tsp

red pepper flakes, 1/8 tsp

large ripe avocados, 2

red bell pepper, 1

cooked fresh lump crabmeat, 3/4 lb

This bright, tangy salad is a lovely way to make a meal of a purchased rotisserie chicken. Or, the next time you roast a chicken, roast two so that you'll have leftovers for this salad. Between the mangos, the red onion, the leafy green romaine, and the nuts, this salad is chock-full of health-enhancing and disease-fighting antioxidants.

chicken & mango salad
with chutney vinaigrette

Thinly slice onion half lengthwise. Rinse onion under cold running water and drain well. Peel mangos with a vegetable peeler, cut flesh away from seed, and cut flesh into 1-inch chunks. Put onion and mangos in a large bowl with chicken, celery, and lettuce.

In a food processor, combine oil, vinegar, mustard, and chile oil (if using) and process until blended. Add garlic and chutney and process until puréed.

Pour dressing over salad and toss gently. Serve at once, or chill for up to 4 hours and mix well before serving. Garnish salad with cashews just before serving.

4 SERVINGS • SOURCE OF VITAMINS • SOURCE OF FIBER

red onion, ½

ripe mangos, 2

cooked chicken, 4 cups shredded

celery, 2 stalks, thinly sliced

romaine lettuce, 4 cups sliced crosswise

peanut or grape seed oil, ⅓ cup

champagne vinegar, ¼ cup

Dijon mustard, 1 Tbsp

Asian chile oil, 2–3 tsp (optional)

garlic, 2 large cloves, finely chopped

mango chutney, ½ cup

toasted cashews, ½ cup

Ripe, sweet melon, marinated in citrus juices and mint and paired with simple grilled shrimp, makes a gorgeous and refreshing summer meal. Watermelon is high in lycopene, an antioxidant found in red plant foods and a popular subject of research due to its apparent power to prevent disease.

watermelon & feta salad
with grilled shrimp

orange juice, 3 Tbsp

lime juice, 4 Tbsp

salt and freshly ground pepper

seedless watermelon, 3 lb

fresh mint leaves, 2 Tbsp
lightly packed

large shrimp, 1 lb, shelled
and deveined

olive oil, 1 Tbsp

feta cheese, ½ cup crumbled

In a large bowl, combine orange juice, 2 Tbsp lime juice, and ⅛ tsp salt.

Cut watermelon into quarters and remove rind. Cut fruit into 1-inch pieces and add to juice mixture. Cut mint leaves lengthwise into thin strips. Add to bowl and stir gently to mix well. Cover and chill for 1–4 hours.

Sprinkle shrimp lightly with salt and pepper. Put in a bowl and add olive oil and remaining 2 Tbsp lime juice. Chill for 30 minutes.

Heat a grill to high, and oil rack. Drain shrimp and thread onto flat metal skewers. Grill shrimp, turning once, until bright pink and opaque, 4–5 minutes total.

Gently stir feta into watermelon mixture. Spoon onto plates and push grilled shrimp off skewers onto salad. Serve at once.

4 SERVINGS • SOURCE OF OMEGA-3S • SOURCE OF VITAMINS

pomegranates

One of the earliest cultivated fruits, juicy red pomegranates are native to the Mediterranean Middle East and are a truly seasonal pleasure, available from fall to early winter. This ancient fruit has gained attention lately for its antioxidant power, but juicy pomegranates are also good sources of vitamin C, potassium, and fiber.

Pomegranates have a leathery peel on the outside and an inedible white membrane within that holds juicy, berrylike seed sacs called "arils" with crunchy edible seeds at their centers. Ruby red, with a deliciously sweet-tart flavor, pomegranate seeds are eaten fresh, and add color and crunch to salads and fruit compotes.

Once you master the technique of seeding pomegranates, the rewards are well worth the effort. To remove the seeds, cut thin slices off the top and bottom of the pomegranate. Lightly score the skin lengthwise in four or five places. Submerge the pomegranate in a bowl of cold water and peel away the skin. Gently separate the fruit into sections, and extract the seeds from the white pith and membrane with your fingers. Discard the pieces of pith and membrane that float to the top, and drain the seeds.

chopped cucumber salad
with pomegranate, feta & mint

In a large bowl, mix lemon juice and olive oil to make a dressing. Slice cucumbers into rounds ⅛ inch thick. Add cucumbers, pomegranate seeds, and mint to bowl with dressing. Mix gently to coat, and season to taste with salt and pepper. Just before serving, gently fold in feta.

4 SERVINGS • SOURCE OF ANTIOXIDANTS • CALCIUM-RICH

lemon juice, ¼ cup

olive oil, 2 Tbsp

English cucumbers, 2

pomegranate seeds, 1 cup

fresh mint leaves, ⅓ cup
coarsely torn

salt and freshly ground pepper

feta cheese, 1 cup crumbled

pear & walnut salad
with pomegranate & blue cheese

In a large bowl, mix vinegar, oil, honey, mustard, ¼ tsp salt, and ⅛ tsp pepper to make a dressing. Add greens, pears, pomegranate seeds, and walnuts and mix gently to coat. Divide salad among 4 plates and top each with about 1 Tbsp blue cheese.

4 SERVINGS • SOURCE OF OMEGA-3S • SOURCE OF ANTIOXIDANTS

cider vinegar, 3 Tbsp

olive oil, 2 Tbsp

honey, 1 Tbsp

Dijon mustard, 1 tsp

salt and freshly ground pepper

mixed baby greens, 8 oz

ripe pears such as Bartlett,
2, cored and sliced

pomegranate seeds, ½ cup

toasted walnut pieces, ⅓ cup

blue cheese, ¼ cup crumbled

Sweet young corn and buttery fresh fava beans are an irresistible pairing in this simple salad. Even after shelling, fava beans have a second skin that needs to be peeled away in all but the youngest, most tender beans. Serve this salad with warm sourdough bread and sweet butter.

fava bean & corn salad
with fresh mint

Bring a large pot of lightly salted water to a boil. Add corn and cook for 1 minute. Remove with a strainer and set aside.

Add fava beans to the pot and cook until just tender, 3–5 minutes. Drain and rinse under cold running water. Slip fava beans from their skins.

In a bowl, whisk together olive oil and vinegar. Stir in corn, beans, radishes, mint, ½ tsp salt, and a few grindings of pepper. Serve immediately, or cover and chill for up to 4 hours.

4 SERVINGS • SOURCE OF MINERALS • SOURCE OF ANTIOXIDANTS

fresh or frozen corn kernels, 2 cups

fresh fava beans, 1½ cups shelled (about 1½ lb)

extra-virgin olive oil, 2 Tbsp

cider vinegar, 1½ Tbsp

radishes, 8, trimmed and thinly sliced

fresh mint leaves, 2 Tbsp coarsely chopped

salt and freshly ground pepper

soup for all seasons

Rich and satisfying or brothy and brightly flavored, soup is the original one-bowl meal. You can combine everything you need in a hearty mixture, from meats and vegetables to pasta, rice, and even cheese. In this chapter you will find soups that use the best produce each season has to offer. Winter calls for savory, warming soups like sherried Vegetable-Lentil Soup or Potato Soup with Kale & Sausage. Spring means bright soups with fresh, sweet flavors, like Sweet Pea Soup with Fresh Sorrel. Tomatoes, whether fresh or roasted, star in summer soups like Roasted Tomato Soup or Tomato & Bread Soup with Fresh Basil. And crisp fall weather heralds the season for hearty soups like Curried Butternut Squash Soup or White Bean & Escarole Soup with Turkey Meatballs. Some of the recipes in this chapter, like Chicken & Wild Rice Soup with Aromatic Ginger, are a nourishing tonic for both body and soul at any time of the year.

Barley is an ancient grain that deserves a larger role in the modern kitchen. It's an excellent source of minerals, especially selenium, as well as dietary fiber that helps regulate cholesterol. Puréeing a little of this rich barley-mushroom soup gives it a creamy texture. If you have a Parmesan rind on hand, add it to the broth as it simmers for a boost in flavor.

savory barley soup
with wild mushrooms & thyme

dried porcini mushrooms, ½ oz

dry white wine, ½ cup

olive oil, 1 Tbsp

shallots, ½ cup chopped

garlic, 2 cloves, minced

fresh cremini mushrooms, 8 oz, chopped

thyme, 1 tsp minced fresh or ½ tsp dried

salt and freshly ground pepper

chicken broth, 3 cups

pearl barley, ¾ cup

tomato paste, 1 Tbsp

lemon juice, 2 tsp

Rinse porcinis well to remove any dirt or grit. In a small saucepan, bring wine to a simmer. Remove from heat and add porcinis; let stand for 15 minutes. Drain porcinis over a bowl, reserving liquid, and finely chop.

Heat oil in a large, heavy pot over medium-high heat. Add shallots and garlic. Cook, stirring frequently, until shallots are wilted, 3–5 minutes. Add creminis, thyme, ¼ tsp salt, and ¼ tsp pepper; cook until creminis release their juices and begin to brown, 4–5 minutes. Add reserved wine and boil, scraping up any browned bits from pan bottom, for 1 minute.

Add broth, barley, tomato paste, 3 cups water, and chopped porcinis to pot. Cover and simmer until barley is tender to the bite, 45–50 minutes.

In a blender or food processor, purée about 1 cup soup until smooth. Return soup to pot, heat until just hot, and stir in lemon juice. Season soup to taste with additional salt and pepper. Serve at once.

4 SERVINGS • SOURCE OF FIBER • SOURCE OF MINERALS

This fresh, pretty soup is everything a good bowl of soup should be: it's comforting, nourishing, and delicious. Look for fresh pea shoots at farmers' markets in early spring. Tender and sweet, they deliver the flavor of fresh peas without the effort of shelling. If pea shoots are unavailable, use the same quantity of baby spinach in their place.

spring vegetable soup
with parmesan & pasta stars

Bring a small saucepan of salted water to a boil. Add pasta and cook until al dente, about 8 minutes or according to package directions. Drain and rinse under cold running water. Set aside. Beat eggs lightly to blend and season with salt and pepper.

Bring broth and 1 cup water to a simmer in a medium saucepan over medium-high heat. Add carrots and simmer, uncovered, until crisp-tender, 5–6 minutes. Add pea shoots and simmer until tender, 2–3 minutes.

Remove pan from heat and slowly drizzle in beaten egg, stirring soup gently in one direction as you pour. Gently stir in pasta and Parmesan cheese and season to taste with salt and pepper. Serve at once.

4 SERVINGS • SOURCE OF VITAMINS • SOURCE OF MINERALS

salt and freshly ground pepper
star-shaped pasta, ½ cup
large eggs, 2
chicken broth, 4 cups
carrots, ½ cup diced
pea shoots, 2 cups chopped
Parmesan cheese, ¼ cup grated

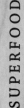

tomatoes

Perhaps no other food evokes summer for cooks as well as the tomato. This native American fruit, introduced to Europe in the sixteenth century, was long rumored to be poisonous, based on its membership in the nightshade family. Today, tomatoes are celebrated for their vibrant color, juicy texture, and a flavor that goes from pleasantly acidic when eaten raw to sweet and mellow when cooked. What's more, tomatoes are vitamin C powerhouses; one tomato contains more than half of the recommended daily allowance. Tomatoes also contain fiber, thiamin, potassium, and the antioxidant lycopene.

As any tomato lover can tell you, there is a world of difference between vine-ripened summer tomatoes and the sturdy, flavorless, and often mealy-textured tomatoes available in the supermarket in winter. In the summer months, celebrate tomatoes by buying them at your local farmers' market or produce stand, and use them in some of the recipes in this book. In the winter, good-quality canned tomatoes may taste better than fresh ones. Cooking tomatoes destroys some of their vitamin C, but enhances the absorption of their lycopene, so, for best results, eat tomatoes both ways!

roasted tomato soup
with sweet onion & parsley

Heat oil in a large saucepan over medium-high heat. Add onion and cook, stirring often and reducing heat as needed to prevent scorching, until onion is soft, 7–8 minutes. Add white wine to pan and increase heat to high; boil until liquid is evaporated, 2–3 minutes. Add broth and tomatoes, scraping up any browned bits from the bottom of the pan used to roast tomatoes, and bring to a simmer. Cover and simmer for 10 minutes to blend flavors.

In a blender or food processor, purée soup, in batches if necessary, until smooth. Alternatively, pass the soup through a food mill. Taste and season with salt and pepper. Ladle soup into bowls, garnish with parsley, and serve with toasted sourdough, if desired.

4–6 SERVINGS • SOURCE OF ANTIOXIDANTS • SOURCE OF VITAMINS

olive oil, 1 Tbsp

sweet onion, 1, chopped

dry white wine, ½ cup

chicken broth, 3 cups

Roasted Tomatoes (page 269)

salt and freshly ground pepper

fresh parsley, 2 Tbsp chopped

sourdough toast, for serving (optional)

tomato & bread soup
with fresh basil

Preheat oven to 350°F. Spread bread cubes on a baking sheet. Bake until dry and lightly toasted, 15–20 minutes. Place in a large bowl and set aside.

Heat oil in a large pot over medium heat. Add garlic and cook until fragrant but not browned, about 45 seconds. Add tomatoes, including any juices, and broth. Season well to taste with salt and pepper, cover, and simmer for 15 minutes, stirring occasionally.

Stir croutons and basil into soup and simmer uncovered for 2–3 minutes, stirring to break up bread. Spoon into bowls and serve at once.

4 SERVINGS • SOURCE OF ANTIOXIDANTS • SOURCE OF VITAMINS

slightly stale artisan-style bread, 3 slices about ½ inch thick, cubed

olive oil, 2 Tbsp

garlic, 2 cloves, minced

tomatoes, 3 lb, cored and diced (juices reserved)

chicken broth, 2 cups

salt and freshly ground pepper

fresh basil leaves, ½ cup torn

Depending on how fresh they are, peas can vary greatly in how long they take to cook. If you can taste before you buy, choose peas that are tender and sweet rather than starchy. Crème fraîche, a cultured cream, adds a silky smoothness and tart flavor to the soup, while sorrel gives it a fresh, lemony tang. If you can't find sorrel, use lemon basil or regular basil.

sweet pea soup
with fresh sorrel

green peas in the pod, 3 lb
(3 cups shelled)

chicken broth, 3½ cups

olive oil, 2 Tbsp

leeks, 1 cup thinly sliced
(white and pale green parts only)

salt and freshly ground pepper

fresh sorrel leaves, ½ cup packed

crème fraîche, ¼ cup

Shell peas, reserving 3 cups of freshest-looking pods. Rinse pods well and coarsely chop. Combine broth and pods in a saucepan over medium-high heat and bring to a boil. Reduce heat to a simmer, cover, and cook for 15 minutes. Strain broth into a bowl and discard pods.

Heat oil in a large pot over medium heat. Add leeks and ½ tsp salt and cook, stirring frequently and reducing heat as necessary to keep leeks from browning, until softened, 5–8 minutes. Add peas, broth, and ½ cup water and bring to a boil. Reduce heat to a simmer and cook, uncovered, until peas are tender, 8–10 minutes. Stir in sorrel and cook until sorrel is wilted, 1 minute longer.

In a blender or food processor, purée soup, in batches if necessary, until smooth. Season soup to taste with additional salt and pepper. Divide among individual bowls and top each serving with about 1 Tbsp crème fraîche. Or, if you want to serve soup cold, cool it to room temperature, cover, and chill for up to 1 day.

4 SERVINGS • SOURCE OF LEAN PROTEIN • CHOLESTEROL-BUSTER

Two kinds of rice give texture and flavor to this fragrant soup. Wild rice has a nutty flavor and a slightly chewy texture, and is high in fiber and protein. Full of aromatic cold-fighters like ginger, garlic, and cilantro, this soup makes a comforting dish to bring to a friend who is under the weather.

chicken & wild rice soup
with aromatic ginger

In a small saucepan, bring 2 cups water to a boil. Add wild rice and reduce heat to a simmer. Cover and cook until rice is tender, 45-50 minutes. Drain.

Heat oils in a large pot over medium-high heat. Add onion and sauté until softened, 3–5 minutes. Add ginger and garlic and sauté, stirring frequently, for 2 minutes. Add broth, carrot, chicken pieces, white rice, and 2 cups water to pot and bring to a simmer. Reduce heat, cover, and simmer until chicken is no longer pink in the center, about 15 minutes.

Transfer chicken to a plate to cool slightly. Remove meat from bones and dice or tear into bite-sized pieces. Stir chicken into soup along with green onion, cilantro, and cooked wild rice. Season to taste with salt and pepper and serve at once.

6 SERVINGS • SOURCE OF ANTIOXIDANTS • SOURCE OF LEAN PROTEIN

wild rice, ½ cup, rinsed

toasted sesame oil, 1 Tbsp

vegetable oil, 1 Tbsp

yellow onion, 1, chopped

fresh ginger, 1 Tbsp grated

garlic, 2 cloves, minced

chicken broth, 4 cups

carrot, 1, peeled and diced

bone-in chicken breast halves, 3, skin removed

bone-in chicken thighs, 2, skin removed

long-grain white rice, ½ cup

green onion, ¼ cup thinly sliced

cilantro leaves, ¼ cup chopped

salt and freshly ground pepper

This soup is inspired by *caldo verde,* a traditional Portuguese soup made with potatoes and thinly sliced kale. Dinosaur kale, also called Tuscan kale, has flat, narrow crinkled leaves and a sweet, mild flavor compared to other kale. Serve this hearty soup with crusty whole-grain bread and chilled amber ale.

potato soup
with kale & sausage

olive oil, 2 Tbsp

**fully cooked spicy turkey
or chicken sausage,** 12 oz

onion, 1, chopped

garlic, 1 clove, minced

dry white wine, ½ cup

chicken broth, 6 cups

waxy potatoes, 1½ lb, peeled
and diced

salt and freshly ground pepper

dinosaur kale, 1 bunch

green cabbage, 2 cups
shredded

Heat oil in a large pot over medium-high heat. Slice sausage into rounds ¼ inch thick, add to pot, and cook, stirring occasionally, until lightly browned, 3–5 minutes. Transfer to a plate with a slotted spoon. Add onion and garlic to pot and cook, stirring often, until onion is soft, about 5 minutes (reduce heat if necessary to prevent scorching). Add wine and boil, scraping up any browned bits from pot bottom, until almost evaporated, 1–2 minutes.

Return sausage to pot and add broth, potatoes, ¼ tsp salt, and ¼ tsp pepper. Cover and bring to a boil over high heat. Reduce heat to a simmer and cook until potatoes are easily pierced with a fork, about 15 minutes.

Tear out and discard tough center ribs from kale leaves and slice leaves into thin ribbons. Add kale and cabbage to soup and simmer, uncovered, until greens are tender to the bite, 8–10 minutes. Season to taste with additional salt and pepper. Serve at once.

4–6 SERVINGS • SOURCE OF VITAMINS • SOURCE OF LEAN PROTEIN

On a cold night, there's nothing more satisfying than a hearty bowl of soup like this one, chock-full of bright vegetables and tender lentils. Unlike other dried legumes, lentils need no presoaking, and they cook relatively quickly. For a vegetarian version of this soup, use vegetable broth instead of chicken.

vegetable-lentil soup
with a touch of sherry

Pick over lentils to remove misshapen ones, rinse, and drain.

Heat oil in a large pot over medium-high heat. Add onion and cook, stirring frequently, until soft, about 5 minutes. Add garlic, carrot, and bell pepper and cook for 3 minutes more.

Stir in broth, lentils, tomatoes, paprika, cumin, ½ tsp salt, and ¼ tsp pepper. Bring to a boil. Reduce heat to a simmer, cover, and cook until lentils are very tender, about 20 minutes. Coarsely chop spinach and stir it into soup. Cook, uncovered, just until spinach is wilted, about 2 minutes. Stir in sherry. Ladle soup into bowls and use a vegetable peeler to garnish soup with shavings of Parmesan.

6 SERVINGS • SOURCE OF FIBER • SOURCE OF ANTIOXIDANTS

brown lentils, 2 cups
olive oil, 2 Tbsp
yellow onion, 1, diced
garlic, 1 clove, minced
carrot, 1, peeled and diced
red bell pepper, 1, cored and diced
chicken broth, 6 cups
diced tomatoes, 1 can (28 oz)
smoked paprika, 1 tsp
ground cumin, 1 tsp
salt and freshly ground pepper
baby spinach leaves, 4 oz
dry sherry, 2 Tbsp
Parmesan cheese, 2-oz piece

peppers

Colorful and sweet bell peppers are native to the Americas. Botanically classified as fruits rather than vegetables, all bell peppers start out green, then ripen into red, yellow, or orange, depending on their variety. The less mature green peppers have a slightly "greener" flavor and contain less of certain nutrients than the ripe red and yellow bell peppers.

A good source of fiber, vitamins, and important antioxidants, bell peppers are deliciously versatile. Eat them raw with dips or chop them into salads. Slice them and add them to stir-fries or pizza. Roasting bell peppers intensifies their mellow sweetness. Bell peppers are generally available year-round, but you'll get a special treat if you buy them from the grower at the peak of their season, late summer through early fall.

Chile peppers, members of the same family, are even more nutritious than their milder cousins, though their intense heat makes it difficult to consume them in volume. Chiles' heat comes from capsaicin, found in the membrane that attaches the seeds to the inside of the fruit. To tame the heat of a chile, remove as much of this membrane and the seeds as possible.

chipotle tortilla soup
with turkey & lime

Purée chipotles in adobo in a blender. Measure out ½–1 tsp and store rest for another use. (Purée will keep for 1 month in refrigerator.)

Heat olive oil in a large pot over medium heat. Add onion and garlic and sauté until onion is soft, about 6 minutes. Add broth, tomatoes, and cumin and bring to a boil. Reduce heat, cover, and simmer for 10 minutes.

Stir in turkey, lime juice, and ½–1 tsp chipotle purée, to taste. Ladle soup into bowls and garnish with tortilla chips, cheese, avocado, and cilantro.

4 SERVINGS • SOURCE OF ANTIOXIDANTS • SOURCE OF LEAN PROTEIN

chipotles in adobo, 1 small can

olive oil, 1 Tbsp

red onion, 1, minced

garlic, 2 cloves, minced

chicken broth, 4 cups

stewed tomatoes, 1 can (15 oz)

ground cumin, ½ tsp

cooked turkey, 2 cups shredded

lime juice, 3 Tbsp

garnish: baked corn tortilla chips, crumbled *queso fresco*, diced avocado, cilantro leaves

roasted red pepper soup
with goat cheese & harissa

Preheat oven to 375°F. Place bell peppers on a large rimmed baking sheet and rub with olive oil to coat, using about 1 Tbsp total. Bake until skins are blistered and peppers soft, 35–45 minutes. Cool, slip off skins, and core and seed peppers. Cut peppers into 1½ inch pieces and set aside.

In a large pot, heat remaining 2 Tbsp oil over medium-high heat. Add onion and garlic and cook, stirring frequently, until onion is soft, 4–5 minutes. Add broth, chickpeas, paprika, cumin, ¼ tsp salt, and bell peppers. Cover and simmer for 15 minutes to blend flavors.

In a blender or food processor, purée soup, in batches if necessary, until smooth. Return soup to pot and stir in vinegar and *harissa* to taste. Ladle into bowls and garnish with goat cheese. Serve at once.

4 SERVINGS • SOURCE OF ANTIOXIDANTS • SOURCE OF MINERALS

red bell peppers, 1½ lb (about 4)

olive oil, 3 Tbsp

onion, 1, chopped

garlic, 1 clove, minced

chicken broth, 4 cups

chickpeas, 1 can (14½ oz), drained

smoked paprika, ¾ tsp

ground cumin, ½ tsp

salt

sherry vinegar, 1 tsp

harissa, ½–1 tsp

fresh goat cheese, 2 oz, crumbled

Fragrant, sweet, and spicy, this butternut soup is spiked with unexpected Thai flavors. Garnish it with the leaves and flowers of Thai purple basil, if you like. Pumpkin may be used in place of the squash; both will give the immune system a powerful beta-carotene boost.

curried butternut squash soup
with coconut & lime

olive oil, 1½ Tbsp

shallots, ¾ cup sliced

fresh ginger, 1 Tbsp minced or grated

garlic, 1 clove, minced

butternut squash, 9 cups peeled and cubed (about 3 lb)

chicken or vegetable broth, 3 cups

salt

Thai red curry paste, 1 tsp

light coconut milk, ¾ cup

lime juice, 2 tsp

Heat oil in a large pot over medium heat. Add shallots and cook until softened, 2–3 minutes. Add ginger and garlic and cook until fragrant but not browned, about 1 minute longer. Add squash, broth, and ½ tsp salt and bring to a boil over high heat. Reduce heat to maintain a simmer, cover, and cook until squash is tender when pierced with a fork, about 20 minutes. Cool slightly.

Put curry paste in a small bowl and stir in coconut milk until well blended.

In a blender or food processor, purée soup, in batches if necessary, until smooth. Return to pot and stir in coconut milk mixture. Heat soup just until hot, stir in lime juice, and season to taste with additional salt. Serve.

4 SERVINGS • SOURCE OF VITAMINS • SOURCE OF FIBER

Ground turkey is often a combination of white and dark meat. For this soup, ask the butcher for only the dark meat. It is a little higher in fat, but turkey is relatively lean compared to other poultry and meat, and the dark meat is more flavorful and higher in iron to boot. Serve this soup with a loaf of warm, crusty artisan bread.

white bean & escarole soup
with turkey meatballs

Line a baking sheet with foil or parchment paper. In a large bowl, mix turkey with egg, Parmesan, bread crumbs, ¼ tsp salt, and ⅛ tsp pepper until well blended. Shape into 1-inch meatballs and arrange about ½ inch apart on prepared baking sheet. Chill for 30 minutes.

Preheat oven to 375°F. Bake meatballs until firm to the touch and no longer pink in center, 16–20 minutes. Meanwhile, drain and rinse beans. Tear escarole leaves into bite-sized pieces and set aside.

In a large pot, heat oil over medium-high heat. Add onion and sauté until softened, about 5 minutes. Add garlic and thyme. Cook, stirring frequently, until fragrant but not browned, 1–2 minutes more. Add wine and boil until mostly evaporated, 2–3 minutes.

Add broth and bring to a simmer. Add beans and escarole and cook until escarole is wilted, 5–7 minutes. Add meatballs and cook until heated through, 1–2 minutes. Ladle soup into bowls and garnish with Parmesan shavings. Serve at once.

4 SERVINGS • IRON-RICH • SOURCE OF FIBER

ground turkey, 1 lb

large egg, 1

Parmesan cheese, ¼ cup grated, plus shavings for garnish

dried bread crumbs, 2 Tbsp

salt and freshly ground pepper

white beans, 2 cans (14 ½ oz each)

escarole, 1 head

olive oil, 2 Tbsp

yellow onion, 1, finely chopped

garlic, 2 cloves, minced

dried thyme, ¼ tsp

dry white wine, ½ cup

chicken broth, 4 cups

seafood for dinner

There are as many reasons to make fish and seafood part of your diet as there are fish to choose from. Fish and shellfish are good sources of high-quality protein, beneficial omega-3 fatty acids, and many key vitamins and minerals, and they are generally low in saturated fat to boot. As an added bonus, most fish and seafood are quick to prepare. Salmon, celebrated for its big flavor and meaty texture, is the star of dishes like Salmon Burgers with Shaved Fennel & Olive Tapenade and Red Curry Salmon in Parchment Packets. Moist, delicately flavored halibut is delicious braised with summer vegetables and tiny orzo pasta, or grilled and topped with mango salsa for a quick weeknight supper. In the summertime you can feast on flavorful trout, panfried and served over a salad of corn bread and heirloom tomatoes, while in wintertime you can keep warm with a hearty Fish & Shellfish Stew, made in the traditional Greek style with bright saffron.

For this whole-grain take on bread salad, use a combination of red, yellow, and zebra heirloom tomatoes, if you can find them. Some markets sell prepared corn bread. If yours doesn't, bake a 9-inch square of corn bread using the recipe given on page 268, your favorite recipe, or a good purchased mix.

panfried trout
with warm corn bread salad

corn bread, about 5 cups 1-inch cubes (page 268)

extra-virgin olive oil, 3 Tbsp

red wine vinegar, 2 Tbsp

salt and freshly ground pepper

ripe heirloom tomatoes, 1½ lb

red onion, ½ cup finely chopped

trout fillets with skin, 4

fresh parsley leaves, 6 Tbsp chopped

Preheat oven to 350°F. Spread corn bread cubes on a large baking sheet. Bake until dry and lightly toasted, 15–20 minutes. Set aside.

In a bowl, mix 2 Tbsp olive oil, vinegar, ½ tsp salt, and a few grindings of pepper to make a dressing. Slice tomatoes in half crosswise and gently remove seeds with your fingers. Chop into 1-inch pieces and add to dressing along with onion. Let tomatoes marinate while you cook trout.

Sprinkle trout lightly with salt and pepper. Heat remaining 1 Tbsp oil in a large frying pan over medium-high heat. Cooking in batches if necessary, place trout skin side up in pan and cook until fish is browned on first side, 2–3 minutes. Turn with a wide spatula, reduce heat, and cook until fish is barely opaque in center, 2–4 minutes longer. Transfer trout to a plate and cover with foil to keep warm.

In a large bowl, combine tomato mixture and parsley with corn bread and mix gently. Divide corn bread salad among individual plates and top each with a trout fillet. Serve at once.

4 SERVINGS • SOURCE OF OMEGA-3S • SOURCE OF VITAMINS

These quick, juicy salmon burgers are a delicious way to get your omega-3 fatty acids—and more. In addition to its delicate anise flavor and delightful crispness, fennel offers a unique array of antioxidants and vitamins that reduce inflammation, boost the immune system, and help prevent disease.

salmon burgers
with shaved fennel & olive tapenade

Remove skin and bones from salmon and cut into 1-inch pieces. In a food processor, pulse salmon with mayonnaise, mustard, shallot, tarragon, ¼ tsp salt, and ⅛ tsp pepper until finely chopped. Stir in bread crumbs. Divide mixture into quarters and shape each portion into a patty.

Heat 1 Tbsp oil in a large nonstick frying pan over medium heat. Add salmon burgers and cook, turning once, until browned on both sides and opaque in center, about 8 minutes total.

Combine greens and fennel in a bowl and toss to coat with remaining ½ Tbsp olive oil and vinegar.

Spread bottom half of each roll with about 1 Tbsp tapenade. Top with a salmon burger, mound about ½ cup of greens mixture on top of burger, and top with other half of roll. Serve at once.

4 SERVINGS • SOURCE OF GOOD FATS • SOURCE OF FIBER

salmon fillet, 1¼ lb

mayonnaise, 1 Tbsp

Dijon mustard, 1 Tbsp

shallot, 1, minced

fresh tarragon, 1 Tbsp chopped

salt and freshly ground pepper

dried bread crumbs, 2 Tbsp

olive oil, 1½ Tbsp

baby greens, 1½ cups

fennel, ½ cup thinly sliced

rice vinegar, 2 tsp

crusty sandwich rolls, 4

Olive Tapenade, ¼ cup
(page 269)

This beautiful, simply seasoned dish is best made the evening after you visit the farmers' market. Make sure to choose the ripest, juiciest tomatoes for the most flavorful results. To remove fresh corn kernels from the cob, stand the cob upright in a large, shallow bowl and hold it firmly. Starting at the top, use a sharp knife to shear off the kernels close to the cob.

braised halibut
with summer vegetables & orzo

heirloom tomatoes, 2 lb

extra-virgin olive oil, 2 Tbsp

balsamic vinegar, 1 Tbsp

garlic, 3 cloves, thinly sliced

salt and freshly ground pepper

orzo, ½ lb

halibut fillet, 1¼ lb

zucchini, ½ lb

fresh corn kernels, 1 cup

fresh basil leaves, 10, coarsely chopped

Core tomatoes and cut into 1-inch chunks, reserving as much of their juices as possible. Put tomatoes and their juices in a bowl and stir in oil, vinegar, garlic, ½ tsp salt, and a few grindings of pepper. Marinate at room temperature for 30 minutes.

Bring a large pot of salted water to a boil. Add orzo and cook until al dente, 8–10 minutes. Drain, rinse in cold water, and set aside.

Remove any skin from halibut fillet and cut into 4 portions. Halve zucchini lengthwise and cut into half moons ⅛ inch thick. Put tomato mixture, along with its accumulated juices, and ¼ cup water in a large, deep frying pan over medium-high heat and bring to a boil. Add fish and zucchini. Reduce heat to a gentle simmer, cover, and cook for 5 minutes. Stir in corn and continue to cook, covered, until fish is opaque but still moist in center, about 5 minutes longer. Stir in orzo and cook until heated through. Season to taste with salt and pepper. Garnish with basil and serve.

4 SERVINGS • SOURCE OF VITAMINS • SOURCE OF OMEGA-3S

Fish fillets cook quickly and can work with an infinite variety of flavorings and accompaniments. They are also an excellent source of lean protein. Here are four easy and delicious ways to add fish to your meals every week.

4 WAYS WITH fish fillets

salmon broiled with lemon

salmon fillet, 1½ lb (about 1 inch thick)

olive oil, 2 Tbsp

lemon juice, 3 Tbsp

sea salt and ground pepper

paprika, ¼ tsp

lemon slices, for garnish

Remove skin and bones from fillet and cut into 4 portions. Brush both sides of fish generously with olive oil and drizzle with lemon juice. Sprinkle with salt, pepper, and paprika.

Preheat broiler. Broil salmon 4–6 inches from heat source, turning once with a wide spatula, until fish is opaque but still moist-looking in center, 8–10 minutes total. Serve, garnished with lemon slices.

4 SERVINGS • SOURCE OF OMEGA-3S • SOURCE OF ANTIOXIDANTS

cod with honey-miso glaze

honey, 2 Tbsp

miso, 1½ Tbsp

lemon juice, 2 tsp

fresh ginger, ½ tsp grated

cod fillet, 1½ lb

salt

Preheat broiler. Line a rimmed baking sheet with foil.

In a small bowl, stir together honey, miso, lemon juice, and ginger. Remove any skin and bones from fillet and cut into 4 portions. Sprinkle with salt.

Place fish on prepared baking sheet and brush tops with about half of honey mixture. Broil about 6 inches from heat for 4 minutes. Turn fish over with a wide spatula and brush second side with remaining honey mixture. Broil until fish is opaque in center, 3–5 minutes longer. Serve at once.

4 SERVINGS • SOURCE OF OMEGA-3S • SOURCE OF ANTIOXIDANTS

grilled halibut with mango salsa

Peel mangos, cut flesh away from pit, and dice. Put onion in a fine-mesh strainer and rinse under cold running water. Drain well. In a bowl, stir together mangos, onion, chile, cilantro, lime juice, and ¼ tsp salt. Set aside.

Heat a grill to medium, and oil rack. Brush fish on both sides with oil and sprinkle with salt and pepper. Grill fish, carefully turning once with a wide spatula, until opaque in center, 6–8 minutes total. Transfer to individual plates and spoon salsa over.

4 SERVINGS • SOURCE OF OMEGA-3S • SOURCE OF FIBER

large, ripe mangos, 2
red onion, ⅓ cup minced
red Fresno chile, 1, seeded and minced
cilantro leaves, ¼ cup chopped
lime juice, 3 Tbsp
salt and freshly ground pepper
halibut fillet, 1½ lb, cut into 4 pieces
olive oil, 1 Tbsp

roasted bass with carrot purée

Preheat oven to 375°F. Bring broth to a simmer in a small saucepan. Add carrots, cumin, and paprika. Reduce heat to simmer gently, cover, and cook until carrots mash easily with a fork, 20–25 minutes.

Remove any skin and bones from fillets. Sprinkle with salt and pepper. Heat oil in a large ovenproof frying pan over high heat. Place fish in pan and cook until fish is lightly browned on bottom, 2–3 minutes.

Put pan in oven and bake until fish is opaque in center, 8–10 minutes.

Transfer carrot mixture to a blender and purée until smooth. Stir in sherry, lemon juice, and salt and pepper to taste. Spoon purée evenly onto 4 plates and top with fish.

4 SERVINGS • SOURCE OF OMEGA-3S • SOURCE OF VITAMINS

chicken broth, 1½ cups
carrots, ½ lb, peeled and diced
ground cumin, ¼ tsp
smoked paprika, ¼ tsp
striped bass fillets, 4 (6 oz each)
salt and freshly ground pepper
olive oil, 1 Tbsp
dry sherry, 1–2 Tbsp
lemon juice, ½–1 tsp

Aromatic spices like ginger and turmeric are prized in some cultures for their healing properties; here, they give flavor and color to broiled snapper fillet. Serve the snapper on a bed of vinaigrette-dressed shredded green cabbage for a light lunch, or with Jasmine Rice, page 210.

spice-rubbed snapper
with lime & cilantro

Sprinkle snapper with salt and pepper. In a large shallow bowl, mix lime juice, olive oil, chopped cilantro, turmeric, ginger, shallot, and garlic. Add snapper fillets and turn to coat well. Cover and let stand for 30 minutes.

Preheat broiler. Arrange fish on a foil-lined baking sheet. Broil 6–8 inches from heat until fish is opaque in the center, 8–10 minutes. Garnish with cilantro sprigs. Serve at once.

4 SERVINGS • SOURCE OF OMEGA-3S • SOURCE OF ANTIOXIDANTS

snapper fillets, 4 (6 oz each)

salt and freshly ground pepper

lime juice, 2 Tbsp

olive oil, 1 Tbsp

cilantro, 2 Tbsp chopped plus sprigs for garnish

ground turmeric, 1 tsp

ground ginger, ½ tsp

shallot, 1 Tbsp minced

garlic, 1 clove, minced

In this recipe, mussels steam in a fragrant broth of ginger, chiles, and light beer, flavored with Chinese salted black beans. Mussels are an excellent source of minerals, especially selenium and zinc, and are also high in folate. If you like, serve the mussels with rice noodles or cellophane noodles.

beer-steamed mussels
with salted black beans

mussels, 1 lb

red Fresno chiles, 2–3

Chinese salted black beans, 1½ Tbsp

peanut oil, 1 Tbsp

fresh ginger, 1 Tbsp minced

garlic, 2 cloves, minced

Chinese or other lager-style beer, 1 cup

lime juice, 1–2 Tbsp

salt

cilantro sprigs, for garnish

Scrub mussels and debeard if necessary, discarding any that do not close to the touch. Slice chiles into rings and discard seeds. Rinse and drain black beans and finely chop.

Heat oil in a large sauté pan with a tight-fitting lid over medium-high heat. Add ginger and garlic and cook, stirring, until fragrant but not browned, about 30 seconds. Add chiles and black beans and stir for another 30 seconds. Add beer and mussels and cover. Shake pan occasionally and check every minute, removing mussels to a serving dish as they open. Cook until all mussels have opened (discard any that don't open), 4–8 minutes.

Stir lime juice and salt to taste into broth. Spoon broth and chiles over mussels. Top with cilantro sprigs and serve.

2 MAIN OR 4 STARTER SERVINGS • SOURCE OF MINERALS

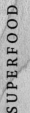

salmon

Salmon ranks as a favorite fish of nearly everyone, and it's no wonder. Admired for its rosy flesh and succulent texture, salmon is also a terrific source of the omega-3 fatty acids associated with heart health. It is also an excellent source of selenium, a trace mineral linked to a decreased risk of cancer. And salmon is a good source of lean protein and myriad other nutrients, including vitamin B12, thiamin, niacin, and potassium.

In addition to being one of the most nutritious and delicious fishes in the sea, salmon is versatile to prepare. It offers an incomparable flavor when served on its own with nothing more than salt and pepper for seasoning, yet is equally suited to bold flavors like the Thai red curry paste and coconut milk used in Red Curry Salmon (opposite). Traditional techniques used to preserve salmon—salting and smoking—also enhance its flavor. Grilled, roasted, poached, and even raw, if there's going to be only one kind of fish on your menu, let it be salmon. Note that studies have shown that farm-raised salmon contains less available omega-3s and more dioxins and other pollutants than line-caught wild salmon, so shop for wild salmon in season.

smoked salmon frittata
with goat cheese & chives

Preheat oven to 350°F. Remove skin from salmon and break into bite-sized pieces. In a large bowl, whisk together eggs, milk, ¼ tsp salt, and ¼ tsp pepper. Gently stir in salmon, goat cheese, and chives.

Heat oil in a 12-inch ovenproof nonstick frying pan over medium-high heat. Pour egg mixture into pan and reduce heat to medium. Cook for 1 minute.

Place pan in oven and bake until frittata is set in the center and slightly puffed up, 25–30 minutes. Cool for 5 minutes in pan, then loosen edges with a spatula and slide onto a large plate. Cut into wedges and serve warm or at room temperature.

8–10 SERVINGS • SOURCE OF MINERALS • SOURCE OF LEAN PROTEIN

hot-smoked salmon, ½ lb

large eggs, 10

milk, ¼ cup

salt and freshly ground pepper

fresh goat cheese, 4 oz, crumbled

chives, 1 bunch, chopped

olive oil, 1 Tbsp

red curry salmon
in parchment packets

Whisk together coconut milk, lime juice, curry paste, soy sauce, and fish sauce. Add salmon, turn to coat, and refrigerate for 30 minutes–3 hours.

Preheat oven to 450°F. Peel and cut ginger into thin sticks. Brush an 18-inch parchment sheet with oil. Place a fillet on one side of sheet, mound ¼ of the bok choy, bell pepper, and ginger on top, and top with 2 basil leaves and 2 Tbsp marinade. Fold parchment over and fold all around perimeter of packet to seal, twisting ends tightly. Place on a baking sheet and repeat to make 3 more packets. Bake for 10 minutes. Remove from oven and cut open packets before placing on plates. Serve immediately.

4 SERVINGS • SOURCE OF OMEGA-3S • SOURCE OF ANTIOXIDANTS

light coconut milk, ¾ cup

lime juice, 2 Tbsp

Thai red curry paste, 1 Tbsp

soy sauce, 1 Tbsp

Asian fish sauce, 1½ tsp

salmon fillets, 4 (6 oz each)

fresh ginger, 1-inch piece

vegetable oil, for brushing

baby bok choy, 12 oz, cut crosswise into 1-inch pieces

red bell pepper, 1, thinly sliced

fresh basil leaves, 8

To accompany this simple, flavorful seafood stew, toast baguette slices, rub them with a raw garlic clove while still warm, and brush them lightly with extra-virgin olive oil. The seafood you use for this dish is completely up to you: try snapper, striped bass, clams, mussels, and shelled, deveined shrimp, in any combination.

fish & shellfish stew
greek style

Toast saffron in a dry frying pan over medium heat until fragrant and a shade darker, about 1 minute. Transfer to a bowl and crumble threads.

Heat oil in a large saucepan over medium heat. Add onion, fennel, and garlic. Sprinkle with salt and pepper and cook, stirring frequently, until vegetables are soft, 6–8 minutes. Add wine and cook until most of liquid has evaporated, about 2 minutes. Stir in broth, tomatoes, potatoes, oregano, and saffron. Season with salt and pepper to taste. Adjust heat to a simmer, cover, and cook until potatoes are tender, about 10 minutes.

If using, scrub clams and mussels well, debearding mussels if necessary, discarding any that don't close to the touch. Cut fish into 1½-inch chunks.

Add clams and mussels to pan, cover, and simmer for 2 minutes. Add fish, cover, and simmer for 1 minute. Add shrimp, cover, and simmer for 5 minutes longer, or until all shellfish with shells have opened (discard any that don't) and shrimp and fish are cooked and opaque throughout.

Remove from heat and ladle into serving bowls. Serve at once.

4–6 SERVINGS • SOURCE OF OMEGA-3S • SOURCE OF LEAN PROTEIN

saffron threads, ½ tsp

olive oil, 2 Tbsp

onion, 1, chopped

fennel bulb, 1 cup trimmed and thinly sliced

garlic, 3 cloves, minced

salt and freshly ground pepper

dry white wine, ½ cup

fish or chicken broth, 3 cups

canned crushed tomatoes, 1½ cups

waxy potatoes, ¾ lb, thinly sliced

dried oregano, ½ tsp

assorted shellfish and fish fillets, 3 lb (see note)

Anytime you can, add seeds to your dishes to take advantage of their marvelous benefits. The sesame seeds featured here provide calcium, vitamin E, and amino acids—plus a rich, nutty flavor. If you like, serve this simple dish with cooked greens from pages 158–59 and short-grain brown rice to soak up the delicious juices.

steamed tilapia
with sesame seeds, ginger & green onion

sesame seeds, 2 tsp

toasted sesame oil, 2 tsp

tilapia or snapper fillet, 1½ lb, cut into 4 pieces

soy sauce, 2 Tbsp

fresh ginger, 1-inch piece

green onions, 6, slivered lengthwise (white parts only)

Shake sesame seeds in a dry frying pan over medium-high heat until they are fragrant and a pale golden brown. Pour into a bowl and set aside.

Place a steamer insert in a large, wide pot with a lid. Fill pot with water to just below level of insert.

Lightly oil a heatproof dish that will fit inside steamer (a 9-inch pie dish or cake pan works well for this). Place fish in the dish or pan, overlapping pieces if necessary, and drizzle with soy sauce and sesame oil. Peel ginger and cut into matchsticks. Sprinkle ginger and half of green onions over fish. Set dish in steamer insert and cover pot. Bring water to a boil over medium-high heat and steam until fish is opaque in the center, 10–12 minutes.

Carefully lift dish from pot and sprinkle fish with sesame seeds and remaining green onions. Serve at once.

4 SERVINGS • SOURCE OF GOOD FATS • SOURCE OF ANTIOXIDANTS

lean & mean

Carnivores, rejoice. Even if you're striving to make your meals more healthful, meat is on the menu. In this chapter you'll find smart and delicious ways to prepare leaner cuts of beef, pork, and poultry. Convenient and infinitely versatile, chicken breasts are a weeknight staple. From grilled skewers of chicken marinated in Indian spices to chicken sautéed with a colorful jumble of cherry tomatoes and basil, you'll discover plenty of new ways to prepare this quick-cooking cut. To make your next backyard barbecue a smashing success, try Skirt Steak Salad with Oranges & Arugula or Grilled Flank Steak with Baby Artichokes & Salsa Verde, which pair meat with fresh greens and vegetables for stunning grilled dishes. Pork Tenderloin with Thyme & Figs is a pretty dish for the midwinter table. And Turkey Lettuce Wraps with Southeast Asian Flavors are a fun and casual way to kick off a meal with friends. These enlightened meat dishes are a pleasure to indulge in.

If you like, serve this juicy roasted tenderloin with soft polenta sprinkled with toasted walnuts and crumbled blue cheese. It makes a beautiful wintertime dinner, when dried figs are especially welcome at the table. If you can't find fig jam, honey makes a fine substitute.

pork tenderloin
with thyme & figs

dried mission figs, 12, stemmed and halved

dry red wine, 1½ cups

pork tenderloin, 1–1¼ lb

salt and freshly ground pepper

olive oil, 1 Tbsp

fresh thyme sprigs, 3

fig jam, 1 Tbsp

lemon zest, 1 tsp grated

Place figs and wine in a small saucepan over medium-high heat. Bring to a boil, reduce heat to low, and simmer for 5 minutes. Remove from heat, let stand for 15 minutes, and drain figs, reserving wine.

Preheat oven to 400°F. Pat pork dry. Trim away excess fat and any silvery membrane. Sprinkle with salt and pepper.

Heat oil in an ovenproof frying pan over high heat. Add tenderloin and turn to brown on all sides, about 4 minutes total. Arrange figs and thyme sprigs around pork. Transfer pan to oven and bake until a thermometer inserted into thickest part of meat reaches 155°F, 18–25 minutes.

Transfer tenderloin and figs to a platter. Cover with foil and let rest for 10 minutes. Add wine, jam, and lemon zest to frying pan. Bring to a boil over high heat, stirring to scrape up any browned bits from pan bottom, until mixture is reduced to ½ cup, 4–5 minutes. Remove and discard thyme.

Slice pork diagonally across the grain into pieces ½ inch thick. Arrange figs around pork and spoon sauce over both pork and figs. Serve.

4 SERVINGS • SOURCE OF LEAN PROTEIN • SOURCE OF FIBER

The ingredients may remind you of Thanksgiving, but they make a cool, refreshing summertime salad as well, with raw celery adding crunch. You may not think of celery as especially nutritious, but it's rich in vitamin C and contains compounds that are thought to lower blood pressure and reduce cholesterol. This salad is great as a sandwich spread.

turkey salad
with celery & cranberry

Combine celery, turkey, parsley, green onions, cranberries, yogurt, and mayonnaise in a bowl and mix well. Season with 1 tsp salt and 1 tsp pepper. Mix again and let stand at room temperature for 30 minutes, or chill for up to 3 hours to blend flavors.

To serve, place a lettuce leaf on each of 4 salad plates and arrange salad on each leaf.

4 SERVINGS • SOURCE OF LEAN PROTEIN • SOURCE OF MINERALS

celery, 1 1/2 cups finely chopped
cooked turkey, 2 cups coarsely chopped
fresh parsley, 1/4 cup minced
green onions, 2, minced
dried cranberries, 1/4 cup
plain low-fat yogurt, 1/4 cup
mayonnaise, 2 Tbsp
salt and freshly ground pepper
butter lettuce, 4 large leaves

Tender pieces of chicken marinated in yogurt and Indian spices make a quick and delicious summer meal. Dress a simple salad of sliced cucumbers and red onion with oil and vinegar, and serve the kebabs with steamed brown basmati rice and flatbread or pita warmed briefly on the grill. Or, pair with curried Golden Potatoes & Cauliflower and raita, page 209.

chicken kebabs
with tandoori spices

plain low-fat yogurt, ¾ cup

lemon juice, 1 Tbsp

garlic, 1 clove, minced

paprika, 2 Tbsp

ground cumin, 1 tsp

ground coriander, 1 tsp

ground ginger, ½ tsp

salt, ½ tsp

cayenne pepper, ¼ tsp

boneless, skinless chicken breast halves, 1½ lb, cut into 1½-inch pieces

vegetable oil, for grill

In a bowl large enough to hold the chicken, mix yogurt with lemon juice, garlic, paprika, cumin, coriander, ginger, salt, and cayenne. Add chicken and stir to coat. Cover and chill for 30 minutes.

Heat a grill to medium-high, and oil rack. Divide chicken pieces equally among 4 or 5 flat metal skewers. Grill, turning once, until cooked through, about 9 minutes total. Push chicken from skewers onto plates and serve.

4 SERVINGS • SOURCE OF MINERALS • SOURCE OF LEAN PROTEIN

Pork tenderloin is both tender and lean, so take care not to overcook it. The center of the pork should be just barely rosy when it is done. Chilling the tenderloin in the freezer for about 30 minutes will make it easier to slice the meat neatly into medallions. Serve with a green salad or vegetable.

pork medallions
with romesco sauce

Trim fat and any silvery membrane from tenderloin and slice into rounds ½ inch thick. In a small bowl, mix ½ tsp salt, fennel seed, cumin, and ½ tsp paprika. Rub spice mixture into both sides of pork loin rounds and let stand at room temperature while you make romesco.

In a blender or food processor, combine walnuts and garlic and process until finely chopped. Add bell peppers, 3 Tbsp olive oil, vinegar, remaining 1½ tsp paprika, cayenne, and ¼ tsp salt and process until smooth.

Heat remaining 1½ Tbsp oil in a large frying pan over medium heat. Cooking in batches if necessary, add pork loin rounds to pan in a single layer and cook just until browned on both sides and still faintly pink in the center, about 2 minutes per side. Transfer to individual plates and spoon romesco over meat. Serve at once.

4 SERVINGS • SOURCE OF ANTIOXIDANTS • SOURCE OF LEAN PROTEIN

pork tenderloin, 1 lb

salt

crushed fennel seed, ½ tsp

ground cumin, ½ tsp

sweet smoked paprika, 2 tsp

toasted walnut pieces, ¼ cup

garlic, 1 clove

roasted red bell peppers, 1 jar (8 oz), drained

olive oil, 4½ Tbsp

dry sherry or red wine vinegar, 1 Tbsp

cayenne pepper, ¼ tsp

For best results, pound the chicken to an even thickness before cooking. Place each chicken breast half between sheets of plastic wrap and gently pound with a flat mallet or rolling pin until it is about ¾ inch thick.

4 WAYS WITH chicken breasts

chicken breasts with mustard sauce

boneless, skinless chicken breast halves, 4

salt and freshly ground pepper

***panko* or unseasoned dried bread crumbs,** 1½ cups

olive oil, 2 Tbsp

dry white wine, ¼ cup

chicken broth, ½ cup

honey, 1 Tbsp

whole-grain mustard, 2 Tbsp

Pound chicken to an even thickness, sprinkle with salt and pepper, and dredge in *panko* to coat well. Heat oil in a large nonstick frying pan over medium-high heat, add chicken, and reduce heat to medium. Cook, turning once, until browned and cooked through, 4–5 minutes per side. Transfer to a plate and cover with foil. Add wine, broth, and honey to pan. Bring to a boil, scraping up any browned bits from pan bottom. Boil to reduce sauce to about ½ cup, 3–4 minutes. Stir in mustard and season to taste. Spoon sauce over chicken and serve at once.

4 SERVINGS • SOURCE OF LEAN PROTEIN

chicken breasts with fig relish

balsamic vinegar, 2 Tbsp

shallot, 1 Tbsp minced

sea salt and ground pepper

ripe mission figs, 8 oz, chopped

mint leaves, 2 tsp chopped

rosemary leaves, ¼ tsp minced

boneless, skinless chicken breast halves, 4

olive oil, 2 Tbsp

In a bowl, combine vinegar, shallot, and ⅛ tsp salt. Let stand for 10 minutes. Stir in figs, mint, and rosemary, mashing figs slightly with a spoon.

Pound chicken to an even thickness and sprinkle with salt and pepper. Heat oil in a large nonstick frying pan over medium-high heat, add chicken, and reduce heat to medium. Cook, turning once, until browned and cooked through, 4–5 minutes per side. Transfer to a platter and serve with fig relish.

4 SERVINGS • SOURCE OF LEAN PROTEIN

chicken breasts & cherry tomatoes

Pound chicken to an even thickness and sprinkle with salt and pepper. Heat oil in a large nonstick frying pan over medium-high heat, add chicken, and reduce heat to medium. Cook, turning once, until browned and cooked through, 4–5 minutes per side. Transfer to a plate and cover with foil.

Add shallots and garlic to pan and cook, stirring frequently, until softened, 3–4 minutes. Add tomatoes and vinegar and cook, stirring frequently, until tomatoes begin to soften and split. Stir in basil and salt and pepper to taste. Place chicken on individual plates and spoon warm tomatoes on top.

4 SERVINGS • SOURCE OF LEAN PROTEIN

boneless, skinless chicken breast halves, 4

salt and freshly ground pepper

olive oil, 2 Tbsp

shallots, ¼ cup minced

garlic, 1 clove, minced

cherry tomatoes, 1½ cups, stemmed and halved

balsamic vinegar, 3 Tbsp

fresh basil leaves, ¼ cup torn

chicken breasts with lemon & capers

Pound chicken to an even thickness and sprinkle with salt and pepper. Heat oil in a large nonstick frying pan over medium-high heat, add chicken, and reduce heat to medium. Cook, turning once, until browned and cooked through, 4–5 minutes per side. Transfer to a plate and cover with foil.

Add shallots and garlic to pan and cook, stirring frequently, until softened, 3–4 minutes. Add wine and lemon juice, increase heat, and boil until sauce is slightly reduced, 2–3 minutes. Stir in parsley, capers, and lemon zest. Season to taste with salt and pepper. Place chicken on individual plates and spoon warm sauce on top. Serve at once.

4 SERVINGS • SOURCE OF LEAN PROTEIN

boneless, skinless chicken breast halves, 4

salt and freshly ground pepper

olive oil, 2 Tbsp

shallots, 2 Tbsp minced

garlic, 1 clove, minced

dry white wine, ½ cup

lemon juice, 2 Tbsp

fresh parsley, 1 Tbsp chopped

capers, 1 Tbsp drained

lemon zest, 1 tsp grated

Pumpkin seeds, also called *pepitas,* are nutritional powerhouses full of iron, zinc, B vitamins, vitamin E, fiber, and antioxidants. They bring a rich, earthy note to this slightly spicy pesto. Serve with a baby spinach salad with marinated red onions. Any leftover pesto is delicious spread on chicken or turkey sandwiches with sliced havarti cheese.

grilled chicken
with cilantro–pumpkin seed pesto

hulled pumpkin seeds, ½ cup

cilantro leaves, 2 cups packed

olive oil, 5 Tbsp

lime juice, 3 Tbsp

garlic, 1 clove

serrano chile, ½, seeded

salt and freshly ground pepper

boneless, skinless chicken breast halves, 4 (6 oz each)

Preheat oven to 350°F. Spread pumpkin seeds on a baking sheet and toast until fragrant and just beginning to turn golden at the edges, 8–10 minutes.

In a food processor, purée toasted pumpkin seeds, cilantro, 4 Tbsp olive oil, lime juice, garlic, chile, and ¼ tsp salt with ¼ cup water until smooth, scraping down sides of bowl as necessary.

Heat a grill to medium-high, and oil rack. Brush chicken on both sides with remaining 1 Tbsp olive oil and sprinkle lightly with salt and pepper. Place on rack and grill, turning once, until cooked through, 12–13 minutes total. Transfer chicken to plates and spoon pesto over top. Serve at once.

4 SERVINGS • SOURCE OF VITAMINS • SOURCE OF LEAN PROTEIN

A leaner take on *larb*, the beloved Southeast Asian dish made with ground pork, this seasoned ground turkey mixture is wrapped in a tender lettuce-leaf packet. For a casual dinner, place the cooked turkey and lettuce leaves on the table and let diners help themselves. If you like, serve a salad of shredded carrot and daikon radish, dressed with seasoned rice vinegar.

turkey lettuce wraps
with southeast asian flavors

Heat oils in a large frying pan over medium-high heat. Add green onions, ginger, garlic, and red pepper flakes and cook, stirring constantly, until fragrant but not browned, about 2 minutes.

Add turkey to pan and cook, stirring to break into pieces, until turkey is no longer pink, about 5 minutes. Add soy sauce and vinegar and cook 1 minute more. Transfer mixture to a bowl.

To serve, spoon about ¼ cup turkey mixture into center of one lettuce leaf at a time, top with a few basil leaves or shreds, and wrap lettuce leaf around filling. Drizzle with ½ teaspoon hoisin sauce, or to taste, if desired.

4 STARTER SERVINGS • SOURCE OF LEAN PROTEIN • IRON-RICH

vegetable oil, 1 Tbsp

toasted sesame oil, 1 Tbsp

green onions, ½ cup thinly sliced

fresh ginger, 1½ Tbsp grated

garlic, 2 cloves, minced

red pepper flakes, ½ tsp

ground dark-meat turkey, 1¼ lb

soy sauce, 3 Tbsp

rice vinegar, 1 Tbsp

butter lettuce leaves, 16
(from 2 small heads)

fresh basil leaves, for garnish

hoisin sauce, for serving
(optional)

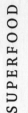

grass-fed beef

Can beef be part of a healthful diet? Absolutely, in moderation. Although most beef is high in omega-6 and saturated fats—unhealthy fats that we enjoy to excess in our Western diets—one way that you can eat well and still enjoy beef is to choose the grass-fed variety.

Typically, grass-fed cattle get more exercise than corn-fed ones as they roam and graze for their natural food, which is one reason the meat of grass-fed cattle is leaner. Additionally, a diet of grass results in more healthful omega-3 fats in the meat of grass-fed beef than in standard corn-fed beef. Grass-fed beef also contains lower residues of hormones and antibiotics than corn-fed beef.

Because of the higher cost of producing it, true grass-fed, free-range beef is significantly more expensive than corn-fed beef. But the price difference is less significant if you take the view that beef is a food to enjoy on occasion rather than something to feast on every day. In the world's healthiest cuisines, beef and other red meats play a modest role on the overall menu. They are enjoyed in smaller portions, perhaps just once every week or two—and they are savored to the fullest.

skirt steak salad
with oranges & arugula

Combine soy sauce, orange juice, 1 Tbsp lime juice, ginger, garlic, and chile paste in a zippered plastic bag. Add steak and refrigerate for 8–24 hours.

Heat a grill to high, and oil rack. Remove steak from bag and discard marinade. Grill steak, turning once, 4–6 minutes total for medium-rare. Transfer to a platter and let stand for 10 minutes.

With a sharp knife, peel orange. Cut in half lengthwise, then slice crosswise into thin half moons. In a large bowl, mix remaining 3 Tbsp lime juice and oil. Add arugula, orange, and radishes and mix well. Mound on a platter. Cut steak across grain into slices ¼ inch thick and arrange over salad. Serve.

4 SERVINGS • IRON-RICH • SOURCE OF ANTIOXIDANTS

soy sauce, ¼ cup

fresh orange juice, ¼ cup

lime juice, 4 Tbsp

fresh ginger, 1 Tbsp minced

garlic, 2 cloves, minced

Asian red chile paste, ½ tsp

skirt steak, 1½ lb, about ½ inch thick, cut into 2 or 3 pieces for ease of handling

navel orange, 1

olive oil, 1½ Tbsp

arugula, 8 oz, stemmed

radishes, 5, trimmed and sliced

beef tenderloin
with sautéed mushrooms

Sprinkle steaks generously with salt and pepper. Heat 1 Tbsp oil in a 12-inch frying pan over medium-high heat. Add steaks and cook until medium-rare, 4–5 minutes per side. Transfer steaks to a platter and cover with foil.

Add remaining 1 Tbsp oil to pan and reduce heat to medium. Add shallots and garlic and cook, stirring, until fragrant but not browned, 1–2 minutes. Add mushrooms and thyme; sprinkle lightly with salt and pepper. Cook, stirring frequently, over medium-high heat until mushrooms have released their juices and begun to brown, 2–3 minutes. Add wine and broth and boil, scraping up any browned bits from pan bottom. Cook until liquid reduces slightly, 1–2 minutes. Spoon mushroom sauce over steaks and serve.

4 SERVINGS • IRON-RICH • SOURCE OF LEAN PROTEIN

beef tenderloin steaks, 4 (each 4–5 oz and 1 inch thick)

salt and freshly ground pepper

olive oil, 2 Tbsp

shallots, 2 Tbsp minced

garlic, 1 clove, minced

cremini mushrooms, ½ lb, sliced

dried thyme, ¼ tsp

merlot or other dry red wine, ¼ cup

chicken broth, ¼ cup

The advent of spring is a good occasion for grilling outside, and this marinated flank steak, grilled alongside baby artichokes and served with a piquant sauce of parsley, garlic, and capers, makes an excellent celebratory dinner. Serve with grilled fingerling potatoes. Flank steak is a lean, flavorful cut with a uniform shape that makes it ideal for grilling.

grilled flank steak
with baby artichokes & salsa verde

flank steak, 1 lb

salt and freshly ground pepper

Salsa Verde (page 269)

lemon, 1, halved

baby artichokes, 1½ lb

olive oil, 1 Tbsp

Sprinkle steak with salt and pepper and rub with 2 Tbsp salsa verde. Cover and refrigerate for 2–24 hours.

Bring a pot of salted water to a boil. Squeeze lemon into water. Trim stems and thorny tips from artichokes. Break off tough outer leaves. Add artichokes to pot and cook until just tender when bases are pierced with a knife, 5–8 minutes. Drain and cool. Halve lengthwise and scoop out prickly choke. Halve again lengthwise. Rub cut surfaces lightly with olive oil.

Heat a grill to medium-high, and oil rack. Wipe excess herbs from steak. Grill, turning once, 5–6 minutes per side for medium-rare, 6–7 minutes per side for medium. After turning the meat, place artichokes on grill, cut sides down, and cook for 4–5 minutes.

Transfer steak to a platter and cover with foil; let rest for 10 minutes. Put warm artichokes in a bowl and toss with 2 Tbsp salsa verde.

Slice steak across grain into thin strips. Arrange on a platter and spoon artichokes over. Pass remaining salsa verde for spooning over steak.

4 SERVINGS • SOURCE OF VITAMINS • SOURCE OF ANTIOXIDANTS

meatless meals

Variety and balance are the appetizing hallmarks of today's meatless main dishes. Because they're not centered around one big protein, vegetarian courses are an opportunity to incorporate a lot of diverse and nutritious elements into a single dish. The flavors of grains, legumes, and vegetables shine when combined with assertive seasonings like ginger, garlic, and chiles. Dishes such as Eggplant & Golden Squash Tagine with Chickpeas & Raisins, simmered in Moroccan spices, and Buckwheat Crêpes with Corn & Roasted Poblano Chiles, flecked with soft, fresh cheese, can hold their own as main courses with vegetarians and non-vegetarians alike. Polenta Lasagna makes a novel main dish for a party or potluck. And Spicy Roasted Cauliflower Pasta or Grilled Tofu Kebabs make simple weeknight dinners. With these satisfying main-dish recipes that are minus the meat but none of the flavor, meatless meals are easier and tastier than ever.

Tangy citrus, dried fruit, and toasted pine nuts flavor this savory Middle Eastern salad. For a meatless picnic spread, pair it with the Roasted Summer Vegetables on page 161 and the Chopped Cucumber Salad with Pomegranate on page 55. It also makes a delicious side dish to accompany simple grilled fish or barbecued chicken.

couscous salad
with saffron, dried fruit & pine nuts

orange, 1

saffron threads, 1/8 tsp

olive oil, 1 1/2 Tbsp

whole-wheat couscous, 1 1/2 cups

dried apricots, 1/3 cup thinly slivered

golden raisins, 1/4 cup

salt and freshly ground pepper

ground cinnamon, 1/4 tsp

fresh mint leaves, 1/2 cup chopped

toasted pine nuts, 1/2 cup

lemon juice, 1/4 cup

Zest orange to yield 1 tsp grated zest. Juice orange and reserve 1/4 cup juice.

Shake saffron threads in a dry frying pan over medium heat until fragrant and a shade darker, about 1 minute. Transfer threads to a small bowl and, when cool, crumble with your fingertips.

In a large bowl, drizzle olive oil over couscous and mix well to coat. Scatter couscous with apricots and raisins.

In a small saucepan, bring 2 cups water to a boil. Stir in saffron, 1/2 tsp salt, and cinnamon and pour over couscous. Cover bowl tightly with foil and let stand until couscous is tender and liquid is absorbed, about 5 minutes.

Remove foil and fluff couscous grains well with a fork. Stir in mint, pine nuts, orange zest, orange juice, and lemon juice. Season to taste with pepper and additional salt. Serve.

4 SERVINGS • WHOLE GRAIN • SOURCE OF FIBER

Originating in the western French region of Brittany, *galettes*, or savory crêpes made with buckwheat flour, can be folded around an infinite variety of fillings. Here they are combined with bright south-of-the-border flavors. These paper-thin whole-grain pancakes are best served right from the pan, but you can make the filling up to 2 days ahead and rewarm it.

buckwheat crêpes
with corn & roasted poblano chiles

Heat oil in a large frying pan over medium heat. Add onion and garlic and cook, stirring often, until onion is softened, 5–8 minutes. Stir in corn and ½ tsp salt and cook just until corn is crisp-tender, 3–5 minutes. Stir in chiles and cook for 1 minute more. Transfer to a bowl and set aside.

In a blender, combine eggs, flours, milk, and butter and blend until batter is smooth, scraping down sides of jar as necessary.

Heat an 8-inch nonstick frying pan over medium-high heat. Brush pan lightly with butter and wipe out any excess with a paper towel. Lift pan from heat and pour ¼ cup batter into hot pan; immediately tilt pan and swirl batter to coat bottom. Adjust heat as you cook crêpe; it should set immediately, forming tiny bubbles. Cook crêpe until edges are lightly browned and surface looks dry, 1–2 minutes.

Turn crêpe with a wide spatula and cook for 1–2 minutes longer. Spoon about ¼ cup poblano mixture onto ¼ of crêpe and top with about 1 Tbsp cheese. Fold crêpe in half over filling, then fold in half again. Serve at once.

8 CRÊPES, 4 SERVINGS • SOURCE OF VITAMINS • SOURCE OF ANTIOXIDANTS

olive oil, 1 Tbsp

red onion, 1, chopped

garlic, 1 clove, minced

fresh corn kernels, 1½ cups

salt

large poblano chiles, 4, roasted (page 269) and cut into ¼-inch strips

large eggs, 3

all-purpose flour, ⅓ cup

buckwheat flour, ⅓ cup

low-fat milk, 1 cup

unsalted butter, 2 Tbsp, melted

cotija **or Monterey jack cheese,** ½ cup crumbled or shredded

This dish has the hallmarks of any memorable pasta dish: a pleasing variety of textures and vivid, complementary flavors. Roasting cauliflower caramelizes it and brings out its sweetness. Seek out true Parmigiano-Reggiano for this recipe; its sweet, mellow flavor is unrivaled.

spicy roasted cauliflower pasta
with garlic bread crumbs

artisan-style bread, 4 slices (each about ½ inch thick)

garlic, 2 cloves, peeled

cauliflower, 2 heads (about 2 lb)

olive oil, 3 Tbsp

salt

whole-wheat penne, ¾ lb

lemon juice, ¼ cup

fresh parsley leaves, ¼ cup chopped

capers, 3 Tbsp drained

red pepper flakes, 1 tsp

Parmesan cheese, ¼ cup grated

Preheat oven to 300°F. Place bread slices on a baking sheet and bake until crisp and dry, about 30 minutes. Rub one side of each slice with a garlic clove. Cool, then tear into chunks. Put in a food processor and process into coarse crumbs. Increase oven temperature to 400°F.

Cut cauliflower into quarters. Discard leaves and cores and cut into slices ¼-½ inch thick. Mince remaining clove of garlic. Put cauliflower in a large baking pan and gently toss with olive oil, ½ tsp salt, and minced garlic. Roast, stirring after 10 minutes, until cauliflower is browned on edges and tender when pierced, about 20 minutes.

Cook pasta in a large pot of salted water until al dente, about 12 minutes or according to package directions. Drain, reserving ½ cup of cooking water. Return pasta to pot and mix with cauliflower, lemon juice, parsley, capers, red pepper flakes, and reserved cooking water. Stir in bread crumbs and cheese and serve at once.

4–6 SERVINGS • SOURCE OF VITAMINS • SOURCE OF ANTIOXIDANTS

White beans, tender squash, and savory onions bake under a crisp blanket of garlic bread crumbs in this spectacular meatless main dish. You can roast the garlic, caramelize the onions, and even assemble the cassoulet the day before you plan to serve it. Feel free to substitute another orange-fleshed squash like kabocha or butternut for the pumpkin.

pumpkin cassoulet
with caramelized onions & roasted garlic

Preheat oven to 375°F. Cut garlic heads in half crosswise and wrap the halves together in a piece of foil. Bake until garlic cloves are soft, about 45 minutes. Cool, then squeeze cloves from cut halves into a bowl, discarding papery skins. Set aside.

Heat 2 Tbsp oil in a Dutch oven over medium-high heat. Add onions and sauté, stirring, until they soften. Reduce heat to medium-low and continue to cook, stirring frequently, until onions are very soft and browned, 25–30 minutes. Reduce heat and stir in a tablespoon of water if necessary to keep onions from sticking. Stir in beans, pumpkin, broth, thyme, 1/4 tsp salt, 1/8 tsp pepper, and reserved garlic.

Cover and bake until pumpkin is tender, about 1 hour. Mix bread crumbs with Parmesan and remaining 1 Tbsp olive oil. Uncover cassoulet (or, if desired, transfer to individual ovenproof serving dishes) and sprinkle bread crumb mixture evenly over top. Return cassoulet to oven and bake, uncovered, until bread crumbs are browned, 10–15 minutes more.

4 SERVINGS • CHOLESTEROL-BUSTER • SOURCE OF FIBER

garlic, 2 heads
olive oil, 3 Tbsp
onions, 2, halved and thinly sliced
cannellini or white kidney beans, 4 cans (14 1/2 oz each), drained and rinsed
baking pumpkin, 2 lb, peeled, seeded, and cut into 1/2-inch cubes
vegetable broth, 1 cup
dried thyme, 1/2 tsp
salt and freshly ground pepper
fresh bread crumbs, 1 cup
Parmesan cheese, 1/4 cup grated

This spicy chili, made mostly from pantry staples, can be doubled easily to feed a crowd. A splash of rice vinegar gives it an unexpectedly bright and zesty flavor. Garnish bowls of chili with grated sharp Cheddar cheese and additional fresh cilantro leaves, if you like.

spicy three-bean chili
with warm corn tortillas

olive oil or canola oil, 2 Tbsp

onion, 1, diced

garlic, 2 cloves, minced

chili powder, 1 Tbsp

dried oregano, 1 tsp

ground cumin, 1 Tbsp

salt, ¼ tsp

diced tomatoes, 1 can (28 oz)

pinto beans, 1 can (14 ½ oz)

white beans, 1 can (14 ½ oz)

black beans, 1 can (14 ½ oz)

rice vinegar, 2 tsp

cilantro, ¼ cup chopped

puréed chipotle chiles in adobo, 1–2 tsp (see Chipotle Tortilla Soup, page 77)

corn tortillas, 16

Preheat oven to 350°F. Heat oil in a large pot over medium-high heat. Add onion and garlic and sauté, stirring frequently, until onion softens, about 5 minutes. Stir in chili powder, oregano, cumin, and salt and cook for 1 minute more.

Add tomatoes, beans, and 2 cups water; bring to a boil. Cover, reduce heat, and simmer, stirring occasionally, for 20 minutes. Stir in vinegar, cilantro, and chipotle purée to taste.

Meanwhile, wrap tortillas in foil and heat in oven until warm. Spoon chili into bowls and serve with tortillas on the side.

6–8 SERVINGS • SOURCE OF VITAMINS • SOURCE OF LEAN PROTEIN

tofu

Tofu is a nutrient-dense, protein-rich staple for much of the world's population. Made from soy milk extracted from soybeans, tofu is packed with heart-healthy fats, soy protein, and phytochemicals called isoflavins, which may help to prevent cancer and heart disease. Some tofu is produced with calcium, making it a good source of that nutrient as well.

If you think of tofu as bland, think again. Tofu is notable for its ability to pick up flavors, making it a blank canvas for your favorite dressings, marinades, and seasonings. Tofu is also available in a wide variety of textures, making it well suited to many different cooking methods.

Firm tofu can be sliced and broiled, cubed and stir-fried, or marinated and grilled. Soft tofu can be puréed into smoothies, or cubed and added to brothy soups. Or, chill cubes of soft tofu and eat them with a drizzle of sesame oil and soy sauce.

The art of making tofu, a centuries-old tradition in Japan, has lately come to the United States. If you ever have the chance to sample fresh soft tofu, don't miss the opportunity; the smooth, mild curds are as creamy and silky as any custard.

grilled tofu kebabs
with spicy marinade

In a bowl large enough to hold tofu, mix soy sauce, vinegar, garlic, chile paste, sesame oil, and orange zest until well blended. Add tofu and mix gently to coat. Cover and chill for 1–24 hours.

Heat a grill to high, and oil rack well. If using wooden skewers, soak in water for 30 minutes. Thread tofu onto skewers, reserving marinade. Grill, turning once and basting frequently with reserved marinade, until browned on both sides, 4–6 minutes total.

4 SERVINGS • SOURCE OF OMEGA-3S • SOURCE OF LEAN PROTEIN

soy sauce, ¼ cup

rice vinegar, 3 Tbsp

garlic, 3 cloves, minced

Asian red chile paste, 2 Tbsp

toasted sesame oil, 2 Tbsp

orange zest, 1 tsp grated

firm tofu, ¾ lb, cut into 1-inch cubes

vegetable oil, for grill

steamed tofu
with greens & peanut sauce

In a blender, combine peanut butter, coconut milk, lime juice, brown sugar, soy sauce, and chile paste and process until smooth. Transfer peanut sauce to a bowl and set aside.

Set a steamer rack inside a large pot filled with a couple inches of water. Place cabbage in rack and bring water to a boil over medium-high heat. Cover pot and steam until cabbage is wilted, about 7 minutes. Place spinach leaves and tofu on top of cabbage. Cover and steam until spinach is wilted and tofu is heated through, about 5 minutes longer.

Mound cabbage, spinach, and tofu on individual plates and drizzle with about 2 Tbsp peanut sauce each.

4 SERVINGS • SOURCE OF OMEGA-3S • SOURCE OF ANTIOXIDANTS

creamy peanut butter, ½ cup

light coconut milk, ½ cup

lime juice, 3 Tbsp

brown sugar, 2 Tbsp firmly packed

soy sauce, 1½ Tbsp

Asian red chile paste, 1½–2 tsp

green or savoy cabbage, ¾ lb, chopped

spinach leaves, 6 oz

firm tofu, 1 lb, cut into 1-inch cubes

These nutty pancakes, which are delicious with a side of sautéed apples or applesauce, also make a nice side dish for roasted chicken or turkey. If you like, you can substitute 1½ cups packaged blended rice mixture for the wild and brown rices in this recipe.

wild rice cakes
with smoked mozzarella & pecans

In a small saucepan, bring 3 cups water to a boil. Add rices, reduce heat to very low, and cover. Cook until liquid is absorbed and rice is tender, 45–50 minutes. Cool rice to room temperature.

In a bowl, beat eggs with a fork until blended. Add cooked rice, cheese, bread crumbs, ¾ cup green onions, pecans, ¾ tsp salt, and ¼ tsp pepper; mix until well blended.

Heat 1 Tbsp olive oil in a large nonstick frying pan over medium heat. With wet hands, squeeze ¼-cup portions of mixture into 3-inch rounds. Place in pan, 3 or 4 at a time, and cook, turning once, until browned and crisp on both sides, 4–6 minutes total. With a spatula, transfer to a plate and keep warm in a 200°F oven. Repeat with remaining mixture, adding more oil to pan as needed.

Place 3 rice cakes on each serving plate. Top with a dollop of sour cream and garnish with green onions. Serve at once.

12–14 PANCAKES, 4 SERVINGS • CALCIUM-RICH • SOURCE OF FIBER

wild rice, ¾ cup

long-grain brown rice, ¾ cup

large eggs, 3

smoked mozzarella or smoked Gouda, 1 cup shredded

fine dried bread crumbs, 6 Tbsp

green onions, ¾ cup finely chopped plus more for garnish

toasted pecans, ¾ cup finely chopped

salt and freshly ground pepper

olive oil, 3 Tbsp

sour cream, ½ cup

Golden layers of polenta take the place of noodles in this colorful meatless lasagna, full of bright vegetables and creamy cheeses. Use stone-ground polenta to get the most nutritional benefit from this ground corn. Unlike most polenta, it retains some of the wholesome germ.

polenta lasagna
with butternut squash & spinach

butternut squash, 6 cups peeled and diced (about 2 lb)

olive oil, 2 Tbsp

dried thyme, ½ tsp

salt and freshly ground pepper

spinach leaves, 12 oz (from about 1 lb spinach)

part-skim ricotta cheese, 2 cups

ground nutmeg, ⅛ tsp

mozzarella cheese, 2 cups shredded

Firm Polenta (page 268)

jarred marinara sauce or Tomato Sauce, 3½ cups (page 269)

Preheat oven to 400°F. In a large baking pan, toss squash with oil, thyme, ¼ tsp salt, and ⅛ tsp pepper. Bake until very tender, about 35 minutes. Transfer to a bowl and mash coarsely with a fork.

Reduce oven temperature to 350°F. Bring 3 cups water to a boil in a large pot. Blanch spinach just until wilted, 1–2 minutes. Drain and rinse in cold water. Squeeze dry and coarsely chop. Combine spinach with ricotta, nutmeg, and ½ cup mozzarella and mix well.

Cut polenta crosswise into thirds and slice each piece in half horizontally. Spoon about ½ cup tomato sauce into a 9-by-13-inch baking dish. Arrange half of polenta pieces in pan, then spoon mashed squash evenly over polenta. Spoon half of cheese mixture evenly over squash and top with about 1½ cups tomato sauce. Top with remaining polenta pieces, then remaining tomato sauce and remaining cheese mixture.

Bake until sauce is bubbling and cheese is melted and golden, about 30 minutes. Let stand for 10 minutes before serving.

8–10 SERVINGS • WHOLE GRAIN • CALCIUM-RICH

The word *tagine* refers to both a gently simmered North African stew and the conical cooking vessel used for stewing meats and vegetables in their own juices. Serve this sweet-spiced stew of eggplant and golden squash over couscous with a dab of *harissa,* the fiery Moroccan chile paste.

eggplant & golden squash tagine
with chickpeas & raisins

Peel and halve squash, scoop out seeds, and cut into 1-inch chunks. Trim eggplants and cut into 1½-inch chunks.

Heat oil in a large pot over medium-high heat. Add onion and garlic and cook, stirring frequently, until onion is soft, about 5 minutes. Stir in *ras el hanout,* turmeric, and ½ tsp salt and cook for 1 minute. Add butternut squash, eggplant, chickpeas, broth, and preserved lemon and bring to a boil. Reduce heat to maintain a simmer, cover, and cook until squash and eggplant are tender, about 20 minutes. Stir in lemon juice and additional salt and pepper to taste.

In a small bowl, mix parsley, almonds, and raisins. Stir ⅔ of parsley mixture into tagine. Sprinkle remaining parsley mixture over top and serve.

4 SERVINGS • SOURCE OF ANTIOXIDANTS • SOURCE OF FIBER

butternut squash, 1½ lb

slender eggplants, 1 lb

olive oil, 1½ Tbsp

yellow onion, 1, chopped

garlic, 1 clove, minced

ras el hanout, 2 Tbsp
(see page 272)

ground turmeric, ½ tsp

salt and freshly ground pepper

chickpeas, 1 can (14½ oz),
drained

vegetable broth, 1½ cups

preserved lemon, ½, rinsed
and chopped (see page 272)

lemon juice, 1½ tsp

fresh parsley leaves, ½ cup
chopped

toasted sliced almonds, ½ cup

raisins or currants, ¼ cup

farmers' market fresh

Fabulous fresh produce, picked at its peak and eaten in season, is one of the keenest pleasures of eating well. Become a regular at your local farmers' market, subscribe to an organic produce box delivery service, or visit a nearby farm that allows you to pick your own produce. In the summer months, you'll be rewarded with the makings of simple, delicious dishes like Marinated Summer Beans with Toasted Almonds & Dry Jack Cheese or spectacular Grilled Cherry Tomatoes with Marinated Feta Cheese. In the cool months, look for colorful root vegetables to make a Gratin of Winter Root Vegetables or Baked Acorn Squash with Lemon & Brown Sugar. In this chapter you will also find a cornucopia of ideas for tasty ways to eat more greens, from Sautéed Brussels Sprouts with Olive Oil & Lemon Peel to Turnip Greens with Bacon and paprika-spiked Creamed Chard with Crème Fraîche.

These crisp sweet-potato oven fries are delicious served with Salmon Burgers with Shaved Fennel & Olive Tapenade, page 89, or Grilled Flank Steak with Baby Artichokes & Salsa Verde, page 124. Use the orange-fleshed sweet potatoes sometimes labeled garnet yams or jewel yams, and choose organic ones if possible, since they are not peeled.

sweet frites
with garlic & sea salt

orange-fleshed sweet potatoes, 2 lb

olive oil, 2 Tbsp

coarse sea salt

Parmesan cheese, 3 Tbsp grated

fresh parsley leaves, 2 Tbsp chopped

garlic, 1 clove, minced

Preheat oven to 450°F. Rinse and dry sweet potatoes. Cut sweet potatoes lengthwise, without peeling them, into slices ½ inch thick, then cut each slice into batons about ¼ inch wide and 3 inches long. Arrange in a single layer on a large rimmed baking sheet and toss with olive oil and ¼ tsp salt. Roast, stirring with a spatula midway through baking time, until tender and browned on the edges, 20–25 minutes.

In a large bowl, mix Parmesan, parsley, and garlic. Add warm oven fries and mix gently to coat. Season to taste with additional salt, and serve at once.

4 SIDE-DISH SERVINGS • SOURCE OF ANTIOXIDANTS • SOURCE OF FIBER

Sweet cherry tomatoes, grilled on aromatic rosemary stems until barely warm, combine with marinated cubes of feta cheese in this beautiful side dish. If you like, use a mixture of red, gold, and green cherry tomatoes. Rosemary's piney flavor makes this dish a good accompaniment to Greek or Middle Eastern fare. Try it alongside Panfried Falafel, page 191.

grilled cherry tomatoes
with marinated feta

Strip all but the very top leaves from rosemary stems, reserving leaves and stems. Mince 1¼ tsp of the leaves. In a bowl, mix feta with 2 Tbsp olive oil, lemon juice, minced rosemary, and a few grindings of pepper.

Heat a grill to medium, and oil rack. Pierce tomatoes with a skewer to make a hole. Thread 3–6 tomatoes onto each rosemary stem. Brush tomatoes with remaining 1 Tbsp olive oil and sprinkle lightly with salt and pepper.

Grill until tomato skins are just beginning to brown and split, about 2 minutes per side. Gently push warm tomatoes from rosemary skewers and mix with marinated feta. Serve at once.

4–6 SIDE-DISH SERVINGS • SOURCE OF VITAMINS • SOURCE OF ANTIOXIDANTS

rosemary stems, 12, each 4–5 inches long

feta cheese, ½ lb, cut into 1-inch cubes

olive oil, 3 Tbsp

lemon juice, 1 Tbsp

salt and freshly ground pepper

cherry tomatoes, 1 lb, stemmed

Simple and versatile, this side dish is essentially a warm broccoli salad dressed with a tangy vinaigrette. This dish may be a revelation to you if you don't care for broccoli boiled or steamed; high-heat roasting brings out a deliciously sweet flavor in this nutritional mother lode. If you buy broccoli tops with the stems already trimmed away, buy 1½ pounds.

roasted broccoli
with pine nuts & balsamic vinaigrette

broccoli, 2 lb

olive oil, 3 Tbsp

salt and freshly ground pepper

balsamic vinegar, 2 Tbsp

Dijon mustard, 1 tsp

toasted pine nuts, ¼ cup

Preheat oven to 400°F. Cut broccoli into 1-inch florets.

In a large baking pan, toss broccoli with 2 Tbsp oil and ¼ tsp salt until well coated. Spread in a single layer. Roast, stirring frequently, until browned and tender, 18–25 minutes.

In a large bowl, mix vinegar, mustard, and remaining 1 Tbsp oil. Add warm broccoli and pine nuts and mix to coat. Season to taste with salt and pepper and serve at once.

4–6 SIDE-DISH SERVINGS • SOURCE OF ANTIOXIDANTS • SOURCE OF FIBER

Cooking greens, like chard and broccoli rabe, are deeper in color than greens used for salads, which indicates that they contain even more vitamins and other nutrients. Adding all forms of leafy greens to your menu is a great way to eat well.

4 WAYS WITH

cooking greens

spicy broccoli rabe with garlic

salt
broccoli rabe, 1 lb, ends trimmed
extra-virgin olive oil, 1 Tbsp
garlic, 3 cloves, thinly sliced
red pepper flakes, ¼ tsp
lemon juice, 1 Tbsp

Bring a large pot of salted water to a boil. Add broccoli rabe and cook until just tender, about 4 minutes. Drain well.

Heat oil in a large frying pan over medium-high heat. Add garlic and red pepper flakes and cook until garlic is fragrant but not browned, 30 seconds. Add broccoli rabe and ½ tsp salt. Stir to coat and heat through, 1–2 minutes. Remove from heat and stir in lemon juice. Transfer to a platter and serve.

4–6 SERVINGS • SOURCE OF ANTIOXIDANTS • SOURCE OF VITAMINS

pan-steamed asian greens

Asian greens (such as bok choy, Chinese mustard greens, or *choy sum*), 1 lb
toasted sesame oil, 2 tsp
garlic, 1 clove, minced
soy sauce, 1–2 tsp

Trim ends of greens and cut crosswise into 1½-inch pieces. Put in a colander and rinse well.

Heat oil in a large frying pan over medium-high heat. Add garlic and cook, stirring, until fragrant but not browned, about 30 seconds. Add greens and ¼ cup water. Cover and cook, shaking pan occasionally, until greens are tender, 3–4 minutes. Remove from heat and stir in soy sauce. Serve.

4 SERVINGS • SOURCE OF VITAMINS • SOURCE OF FIBER

creamed chard with crème fraîche

Tear chard leaves from center ribs and stems. Chop ribs and stems together. Coarsely chop leaves separately.

Heat oil in a large frying pan over medium-high heat. Add ribs and stems and cook, stirring often, for 2 minutes. Add leaves and cook until chard is wilted and tender and any liquid has cooked away, about 3 minutes longer.

In a bowl, whisk together crème fraîche, lemon juice, cumin, paprika, ½ tsp salt, and a few grindings of pepper. Stir into pan and cook until sauce is slightly thickened, 1–2 minutes. Spoon into a bowl and serve at once.

4 SERVINGS • CALCIUM-RICH • SOURCE OF FIBER

red Swiss chard, 1½ lb
olive oil, 2 Tbsp
crème fraîche, ½ cup
lemon juice, 2 Tbsp
ground cumin, 1 tsp
paprika, ½ tsp
salt and freshly ground pepper

turnip greens with bacon

Remove stems and tough center ribs from greens and discard. Coarsely chop leaves.

Heat oil in a large frying pan over medium-high heat. Add bacon and cook, stirring frequently, until beginning to brown and crisp, 2–3 minutes. Add garlic and red pepper flakes and cook for 30 seconds. Add greens, ¼ tsp salt, and 1 cup water. Bring to a boil.

Reduce heat to a simmer, cover, and cook, shaking pan occasionally, until greens are tender, about 10 minutes. Season to taste with additional salt, if desired. Serve at once.

4 SERVINGS • SOURCE OF VITAMINS • CALCIUM-RICH

turnip greens, 1½ lb
olive oil, 1½ Tbsp
turkey bacon, 3 slices, diced
garlic, 2 cloves, minced
red pepper flakes, ⅛ tsp
salt

This vegetable salad, inspired by Spanish *escalivada*, can be served warm from the oven, but is equally delicious at room temperature. If you like, serve with grilled fish or top the vegetables with anchovies, arranging them on the salad as you would on a classic Caesar. Leftovers are delicious cooked into a frittata; see page 99 for guidance.

roasted summer vegetables
with goat cheese

Preheat oven to 400°F. Cut bell peppers, onion, eggplant, and zucchini into 1-inch pieces.

Pour 2 Tbsp olive oil into a large roasting pan. Add vegetables, sprinkle with garlic, cumin, paprika, ¾ tsp salt, and ¼ tsp pepper, and stir until well combined. Roast, stirring every 10 minutes, until vegetables are tender, about 25 minutes total. Drizzle with 1 Tbsp vinegar.

In a large bowl, whisk together remaining 2 Tbsp vinegar and remaining 2 Tbsp olive oil. Add romaine leaves and toss to coat.

Divide romaine among 4 plates, stacking leaves slightly to make a bed for vegetables. Spoon vegetables evenly over romaine and sprinkle about 2 Tbsp goat cheese over each salad. Serve.

4 SERVINGS • SOURCE OF VITAMINS • SOURCE OF MINERALS

red or orange bell peppers, 1 lb
red onion, 1
slender eggplant, 1 lb
zucchini, ½ lb
olive oil, 4 Tbsp
garlic, 3 cloves, minced
ground cumin, ¾ tsp
smoked paprika, ¾ tsp
salt and freshly ground pepper
sherry vinegar or red wine vinegar, 3 Tbsp
romaine lettuce, 1 head, separated into leaves
fresh goat cheese, 4 oz, crumbled

A vibrant reddish purple member of the chicory family, radicchio's fresh, bitter flavor mellows deliciously when it is grilled until tender. A wedge makes a great side dish for grilled meat—try it with veal chops—or it can be sliced and used as a pizza or bruschetta topping or as a sandwich filling.

grilled radicchio
with olive oil & sea salt

radicchio, 2 heads

olive oil, 2 Tbsp

coarse sea salt and pepper

balsamic vinegar, 4 tsp

Quarter radicchio heads lengthwise, leaving cores intact. Brush cut sides generously with olive oil, and sprinkle with salt and pepper.

Heat a grill to medium-high, and oil rack. Place radicchio, cut sides down, on grill and cook, turning frequently, until browned and tender when pierced at the core with a knife, 8–12 minutes total. (Close lid if using a gas grill.)

Transfer to a platter and drizzle each piece with about ½ tsp oil and ½ tsp balsamic vinegar. Sprinkle with additional salt and pepper, if desired. Serve.

4 SIDE-DISH SERVINGS • SOURCE OF VITAMINS • SOURCE OF MINERALS

squashes

Naturally sweet summer and winter squashes are members of the same botanical family and share some of the same nutritional characteristics.

Summer squashes, such as zucchini, pattypan, and crookneck, have thin, edible skins and soft, edible seeds. Summer squashes are high in vitamin C, beta-carotene, and several minerals. They're best cooked simply, steamed or grilled, then eaten on their own or used in soups, salads, and pasta dishes.

Winter squashes, such as acorn, butternut, kabocha, and pumpkin (a cousin of squash, part of the gourd family), have hard skins and dense, sweet flesh. They are rich in vitamin A, vitamin C, and fiber, and their flavor and texture are well suited to a variety of cooking techniques. Peel winter squashes with a sturdy vegetable peeler, cut in half and scoop out the seeds, and then cube the flesh for steaming or roasting. Or, simpler yet, cut whole winter squashes in half, scoop out the seeds, and bake with the skin on until the flesh is tender enough to scoop from the peel. Cooked winter squash makes a silky purée, perfect for adding body to soups, or flavor and nutrition to muffins and quick breads.

grilled squash & orzo salad
with pine nuts & mint

Trim and cut squash lengthwise into slices ¼ inch thick. Put in a bowl and add ½ Tbsp oil, ½ tsp salt, and a few grindings of pepper. Mix to coat.

Heat a grill to medium-high, and oil rack. Grill squash, turning once, until tender, 5–8 minutes total. (Close lid if using a gas grill.) Cool and cut into 1½ inch pieces, and put in a large bowl.

Bring a pot of salted water to a boil. Add orzo and cook until al dente, about 8 minutes. Drain and rinse with cold water. Add orzo to squash along with remaining 1 Tbsp oil, lemon juice, vinegar, and pine nuts. Season to taste with salt and pepper. Just before serving, stir in cheese and mint.

4 SERVINGS • SOURCE OF VITAMINS • SOURCE OF MINERALS

mixed yellow squash and zucchini, 2 lb

olive oil, 1½ Tbsp

salt and freshly ground pepper

orzo, ½ lb

lemon juice, 3 Tbsp

champagne vinegar or white wine vinegar, 1 Tbsp

toasted pine nuts, ½ cup

Parmesan cheese, ½ cup curls or shavings

fresh mint leaves, 3 Tbsp coarsely chopped

baked acorn squash
with lemon & brown sugar

Preheat oven to 425°F. Line a rimmed baking sheet with foil. With a sharp knife, cut each squash in half lengthwise and scoop out seeds. Cut halves into 1-inch wedges and place on baking sheet. Toss with oil to coat, then spread slices evenly on sheet, cut side down. Sprinkle with salt and pepper.

Bake for 15 minutes. Remove from oven and sprinkle with brown sugar. Return to oven and continue baking until squash is tender and sugar has melted and begun to caramelize, about 10 minutes longer. Drizzle squash with lemon juice and use a wide spatula to transfer wedges to a platter. Serve warm or at room temperature.

4–6 SIDE-DISH SERVINGS • SOURCE OF VITAMINS • SOURCE OF FIBER

acorn squash, 2 (about 1½ lb each)

olive oil, 2 Tbsp

salt and freshly ground pepper

brown sugar, ¼ cup firmly packed

lemon juice, 1½ Tbsp

Choose any combination of sweet, nutritious roots for this gratin, including parsnips, sweet potatoes, carrots, turnips, golden beets, and rutabagas. True Parmigiano-Reggiano cheese imported from Italy has a sweet, nutty flavor that picks up the flavors of the nutmeg and the root vegetables, so be sure to seek it out for this dish.

gratin of winter root vegetables
with thyme & nutmeg

Preheat oven to 300°F. Place bread slices on a baking sheet and bake until crisp and dry, 20–25 minutes. Rub one side of each slice of warm bread with one of the garlic cloves. Let bread cool and tear into chunks. Put in a food processor, in batches if necessary, and process until bread forms coarse crumbs. Transfer to a bowl and mix with 1 Tbsp oil and Parmesan. Set aside.

Increase oven temperature to 400°F. Mince remaining clove of garlic. Peel root vegetables and cut into ½-inch pieces. Heat remaining 1 Tbsp oil in a large ovenproof frying pan over medium-high heat. Add vegetables, ½ tsp salt, a few grindings of pepper, thyme, nutmeg, and minced garlic to the pan. Cook, stirring occasionally, until vegetables begin to brown, 4–6 minutes. Add ¼ cup water, cover, and simmer until vegetables are tender when pierced, about 10 minutes.

Remove from heat and, if desired, transfer vegetables to a casserole or baking dish for serving. Sprinkle evenly with bread-crumb mixture. Bake until top is golden brown, 10–12 minutes. Serve at once.

4–6 SERVINGS • SOURCE OF ANTIOXIDANTS • SOURCE OF MINERALS

artisan-style sourdough bread, 3 slices (about ½ inch thick)

garlic, 2 cloves, peeled

olive oil, 2 Tbsp

Parmesan cheese, ⅓ cup grated

root vegetables, 3 lb (see note)

salt and freshly ground pepper

thyme, ½ tsp minced fresh or ¼ tsp dried

ground nutmeg, ¼ tsp

When they are treated right, Brussels sprouts are sweet and tender. One way to bring out the best in them is to cook them quickly, with nothing more than a little good olive oil, lemon, and sea salt. Use the largest frying pan you have for this recipe so that the Brussels sprouts have room to move around and brown as they cook. Serve with pork tenderloin, page 108.

sautéed brussels sprouts
with olive oil & lemon peel

Brussels sprouts, 1 lb

olive oil, 2 Tbsp

lemon zest strips, 1 tsp

sea salt and ground pepper

lemon juice, 3 Tbsp

Trim away stem ends of Brussels sprouts and cut lengthwise into slices ¼ inch thick.

Heat oil in a large frying pan over medium-high heat. Add sprouts, lemon zest, ½ tsp salt, and a few grindings of pepper. Cook, stirring frequently and reducing heat as necessary to prevent scorching, until sprouts are tender and slightly browned, 7–8 minutes. Stir in lemon juice and cook for 1 minute longer. Serve at once.

4 SIDE-DISH SERVINGS • SOURCE OF VITAMINS • SOURCE OF ANTIOXIDANTS

Green and yellow summer beans shine with flavor when cooked until just tender and tossed in a simple dressing of lemon juice and olive oil. Use aged dry Monterey jack cheese if you can find it; it has a sharp, sweet flavor that brings out the sweetness of the beans.

marinated summer beans
with toasted almonds & dry jack cheese

Zest lemon to yield 1 tsp grated zest. Juice lemon and reserve 3 Tbsp juice.

Trim beans, and slice diagonally if desired. Bring a large saucepan of salted water to a boil. Add beans and boil just until tender, 3–4 minutes. Drain and plunge beans into ice water to cool. Drain well and put in a large bowl.

Add olive oil, tarragon, 2½ Tbsp lemon juice, and lemon zest to beans. Mix well and season to taste with salt and pepper and additional lemon juice, if desired. Transfer to a platter, top with cheese and almonds, and serve.

4 SIDE-DISH SERVINGS • SOURCE OF VITAMINS • SOURCE OF MINERALS

lemon, 1
green beans, ½ lb
yellow wax beans, ½ lb
salt and freshly ground pepper
olive oil, 1 Tbsp
fresh tarragon, 2 Tbsp chopped
dry Monterey jack or Parmesan cheese, ½ cup curls or shavings
toasted almonds, ⅓ cup coarsely chopped

mediterranean tonight

The cuisines of the lands bordering the Mediterranean Sea serve as inspiring models for eating well. The region boasts a wealth of naturally healthful ingredients as well as a centuries-old tradition of relishing good food simply prepared. Although the flavors may differ from region to region, whole grains, fresh produce, and olive oil are common elements that make Mediterranean food celebrated for its health-giving properties. In this chapter, you'll find vibrant, casual dishes like Spanish Peperonata with Olives & Capers and Quick-Sautéed Calamari with White Beans & Roasted Peppers, served over tomato-rubbed bread. You'll also find simple, tasty ideas for whole grains and legumes from North Africa and Italy, including Farro Salad with Artichoke Hearts and Bulgur & Lentil Pilaf with Almond Gremolata. Lastly, look for some new twists on old favorites, like Mint Tabbouleh with Sweet 100s and Barley Risotto with Chicken, Mushrooms & Greens.

Often overlooked on the modern table, barley has a pleasantly chewy texture and a sweet, nutty flavor. When stirred into broth over low heat, it cooks into a creamy risotto-style dish. Meaty mushrooms, shredded cooked chicken, and slightly bitter dandelion greens make this a delicious early fall dinner. If dandelion greens are not available, substitute baby arugula.

barley risotto
with chicken, mushrooms & greens

chicken broth, 6 cups

olive oil, 1½ Tbsp

onion, 1, chopped

garlic, 1 clove, minced

cremini mushrooms, 2 cups sliced

salt and freshly ground pepper

dry white wine, ½ cup

pearl barley, 1 cup

dandelion greens, 3 cups bite-sized pieces

cooked chicken, 2 cups diced or shredded

Parmesan cheese, ½ cup grated

In a medium saucepan over medium-high heat, bring broth to a simmer. Turn off heat, cover, and keep warm.

Heat oil in a large saucepan over medium-high heat. Add onion and garlic and cook, stirring frequently, until onion is soft, about 5 minutes. Add mushrooms, ¼ tsp salt, and a few grindings of pepper. Cook, stirring frequently, until mushrooms release their juices and start to brown, 4–5 minutes. Add wine and bring to a boil for 1 minute.

Add 5 cups of hot broth and the barley. Cover and simmer over medium-low heat, stirring occasionally and adding more broth ¼ cup at a time if barley becomes dry, until barley is tender, about 45 minutes.

Stir in dandelion greens and more broth, if necessary. Cook, uncovered, until greens are wilted, about 2 minutes. Stir in chicken and cook for 1 minute to heat through. Stir in Parmesan and season to taste with additional salt and pepper. Serve at once.

4 SERVINGS • WHOLE GRAIN • SOURCE OF MINERALS

This colorful mélange of sweet bell peppers stewed in olive oil is delicious served warm or at room temperature. It makes a nice addition to a Spanish tapas feast: Serve with serrano ham or slices of chorizo, spicy roasted potatoes, and a chilled rosé. The peppers are also delicious on grilled bread as an appetizer or served alongside cold roast chicken for a picnic.

spanish peperonata
with olives & capers

Core and seed bell peppers and cut into 1½-inch pieces.

Heat olive oil in a large frying pan over medium-high heat. Add shallots and garlic and cook, stirring, until fragrant but not browned, 1–2 minutes. Add bell peppers, ¼ tsp salt, and a few grindings of pepper and cook, stirring frequently, until bell peppers are soft, about 8 minutes. Add vinegar, olives, and capers and cook until most of the liquid has evaporated, 1–2 minutes longer. Season to taste with additional salt and pepper. Serve.

6–8 SERVINGS • SOURCE OF ANTIOXIDANTS • SOURCE OF VITAMINS

red, yellow, and/or orange bell peppers, 2 lb

olive oil, 3 Tbsp

shallots, ½ cup thinly sliced

garlic, 1 clove, minced

salt and freshly ground pepper

sherry vinegar, ¼ cup

mild green olives, ¼ cup pitted and coarsely chopped

capers, 1 Tbsp, drained

Here is a fresh take on a classic Middle Eastern salad: With aromatic fresh mint standing in for the usual parsley, tabbouleh becomes a perfect partner to simple broiled lamb chops. Bulgur is a sturdy, chewy form of wheat that becomes delightfully juicy and flavorful when dressed with good olive oil and vinegar and tossed with tiny, sweet cherry tomatoes.

mint tabbouleh
with sweet 100s

bulgur, 1 cup

sweet 100 cherry tomatoes, 2 cups

lemon juice, 3 Tbsp

extra-virgin olive oil, 3 Tbsp

balsamic or aged red wine vinegar, 1 Tbsp

salt and freshly ground pepper

fresh mint leaves, ½ cup packed, coarsely chopped

English cucumber, ½ cup seeded and chopped

green onions, ⅓ cup thinly sliced

Put bulgur in a bowl. Bring 1 cup water to a boil. Pour over bulgur, cover bowl tightly with foil, and let stand for 30 minutes.

Stem tomatoes and cut about 1 cup of them in half. In a large bowl, mix lemon juice, olive oil, vinegar, ¼ tsp salt, and a few grindings of pepper. Add halved and whole tomatoes. Drain any remaining water from bulgur and add bulgur to tomato mixture along with mint, cucumber, and green onions. Season to taste with additional salt and pepper and serve, or cover and chill for up to 1 day.

4 SERVINGS • WHOLE GRAIN • SOURCE OF FIBER

wheat

There's a good reason that wheat is often referred to as the "staff of life": Wheat is a sustaining staple for much of the world. Whole-wheat flour is a source of complex carbohydrates, which are the body's main fuel for energy. Whole wheat also contains thiamine, niacin, selenium, and magnesium, all essential nutrients that support good health.

A member of the grass family, wheat kernels are most commonly ground into flour and made into other products. By far the most notable of these is bread, in which wheat's high gluten content allows the proteins to stretch as the bread rises and develops a tender, airy texture.

Beyond the bread aisle, whole wheat is showing up on grocery store shelves in an increasing variety of dried pasta. Whole-wheat pasta has a pleasantly nutty flavor and is slightly more sturdy than regular pasta, which makes it especially well suited to sauces with bold flavors and chunky textures.

To enjoy wheat in a more intact form, try farro, a variety of wheat commonly enjoyed as a whole grain in Italy, or bulgur, another cereal form of wheat favored in Turkey and the Levant.

farro salad
with artichoke hearts

Rinse farro and put in a medium saucepan with 2 ½ cups water; bring to a boil. Reduce heat, cover, and simmer until grains are tender and water is absorbed, about 25 minutes.

Drain tomatoes before cutting into julienne, reserving oil to use in place of some of the olive oil, if you like. Drain, rinse, and quarter artichokes.

In a large bowl, whisk together vinegar and olive oil. Add cooked farro, sun-dried tomatoes, artichoke hearts, onion, parsley, and pine nuts and mix well. Season generously to taste with salt and pepper, and serve.

4–6 SERVINGS • WHOLE GRAIN • SOURCE OF VITAMINS

semi-pearled farro, 1 ¼ cups

oil-packed sun-dried tomatoes, ¼ cup packed

artichoke hearts, 1 jar (14 oz)

red wine vinegar, 6 Tbsp

olive oil, 3 Tbsp

red onion, ½ cup finely chopped, rinsed

parsley leaves, ½ cup chopped

toasted pine nuts, ½ cup

salt and freshly ground pepper

bulgur & lentil pilaf
with almond gremolata

In a small saucepan, cover lentils with water and simmer until tender but firm to the bite, about 20 minutes. Drain.

Heat oil in a large frying pan over medium-high heat. Add onion and garlic and cook, stirring often, until onion is wilted, 3–5 minutes. Stir in bulgur, coriander, ¼ tsp salt, and ¼ tsp ground pepper. Cook for 1 minute. Stir in lentils and broth and bring to a boil. Reduce heat to low, cover, and simmer for 5 minutes. Remove from heat and let stand, covered, for 15 minutes. Put almonds, parsley, and lemon zest together on a board and coarsely chop. Fluff pilaf with a fork and stir in lemon juice. Season to taste with salt and pepper. Spoon pilaf onto a platter and sprinkle with almond mixture.

4 SERVINGS • WHOLE GRAIN • SOURCE OF MINERALS

brown lentils, ¾ cup, picked over, rinsed, and drained

olive oil, 2 Tbsp

onion, 1, chopped

garlic, 2 cloves, minced

bulgur, 1 cup

ground coriander, 1 tsp

salt and freshly ground pepper

vegetable broth or water, 2 cups

toasted almonds, ¼ cup

fresh parsley leaves, ⅓ cup

lemon zest, 1 Tbsp grated

lemon juice, 2 Tbsp

Green French lentils have a nutty, peppery flavor and a firm texture that holds up well to cooking and marinating. This flavorful legume salad makes a delicious accompaniment to the Salmon Broiled with Lemon on page 92—a classic pairing—or a simple roast chicken.

green lentil salad
with red peppers & shallots

Pick over lentils to remove misshapen ones, rinse, and drain. Bring a medium pot of water to a boil. Add lentils, reduce heat, and simmer until lentils are tender to the bite, 18–25 minutes.

While the lentils cook, heat 2 Tbsp oil in large nonstick frying pan over medium-high heat. Add shallots and cook until softened, 2–3 minutes. Reduce heat and cook, stirring frequently, until shallots are browned, 5–8 minutes longer. Set aside.

Drain lentils and put in a bowl. Stir in peppers, vinegar, parsley, ½ tsp salt, shallots, and remaining 1 Tbsp olive oil.

Serve warm or at room temperature, stirring well before serving.

4 SERVINGS • CHOLESTEROL-BUSTER • SOURCE OF MINERALS

small green or brown lentils, 1 cup

extra-virgin olive oil, 3 Tbsp

shallots, 1½ cups thinly sliced

roasted red peppers, ½ cup, cut into strips

sherry vinegar, 3½ Tbsp

fresh parsley leaves, 3 Tbsp coarsely chopped

salt

To save time, use good-quality jarred roasted peppers and canned beans in this saucy, Spanish-inspired dish. Once all the ingredients simmer together, the shortcut will be unnoticeable and the results delicious. Pair with Roasted Summer Vegetables, page 161, and Pork Medallions with Romesco Sauce, page 115, for a tempting small plates spread.

quick-sautéed calamari
with white beans & roasted peppers

cleaned squid rings and tentacles, 1 lb

salt and freshly ground pepper

olive oil, 3 Tbsp

red onion, ¾ cup minced

garlic, 2 cloves, minced

chicken broth, ½ cup

cannellini beans, 2 cans (14 ½ oz each), drained

roasted red bell peppers, 1 cup, cut into strips

sherry vinegar, 2 Tbsp

fresh parsley, ½ cup chopped

crusty artisan-style bread, 8 slices

large ripe tomato, 1

Sprinkle squid with salt and pepper. Heat a large nonstick frying pan over medium-high heat. Add 1 Tbsp oil and heat until hot. Add squid and stir just until opaque, 1–2 minutes. Transfer squid to a bowl and set aside.

Add another 1 Tbsp oil to pan and add onion and garlic. Cook, stirring frequently and reducing heat as necessary to prevent scorching, until onion is wilted, 3–5 minutes. Add broth, beans, bell peppers, and vinegar. Simmer, uncovered, for 2–3 minutes to blend flavors. Stir squid back into pan along with parsley and cook just until heated through. Season to taste with salt and pepper.

Just before serving, toast bread slices and slice tomato in half crosswise. Brush one side of each piece of bread with remaining 1 Tbsp olive oil. Rub cut side of tomato over bread. Place a bread slice on each plate and spoon squid mixture over bread. Serve at once.

4 SERVINGS • SOURCE OF LEAN PROTEIN • SOURCE OF FIBER

Next time you're looking for a quick side dish to round out a meal, skip the rice or potatoes and head to the pantry for beans! The canned version of any bean can be quickly dressed up to rival the flavors of long-simmered dried beans.

beans & lentils

lentils with garlic & herbs

green lentils, 1 cup

garlic, 1 clove, peeled and smashed

lemon juice, 3 Tbsp

extra-virgin olive oil, 2 Tbsp

mixed fresh herbs, such as tarragon, sage, thyme, and parsley, 3 Tbsp chopped

salt and freshly ground pepper

Pick over lentils to remove misshapen ones, rinse, and drain. Put in a medium saucepan with water to cover. Add garlic and bring to a boil.

Reduce heat to maintain a simmer and cook until lentils are tender but still firm to the bite, about 20 minutes. Drain well and pour into a bowl.

Stir in lemon juice, oil, and herbs. Season to taste with salt and pepper.

4 SERVINGS • SOURCE OF FIBER • SOURCE OF LEAN PROTEIN

beans with sage & pancetta

olive oil, 1 Tbsp

pancetta, 1 oz, diced

garlic, 2 cloves, peeled and smashed

borlotti or kidney beans, 2 cans (14½ oz each), rinsed and drained

chicken broth, 1 cup

fresh sage leaves, 6–8, torn

salt and freshly ground pepper

Heat oil in a medium saucepan over medium-high heat. Add pancetta and cook until beginning to brown, about 2 minutes. Add garlic and cook until fragrant but not browned, about 30 seconds. Add beans, broth, and sage. Reduce heat to medium-low, cover, and simmer for 8–10 minutes to blend flavors. Season to taste with salt and pepper.

4 SERVINGS • IRON-RICH • SOURCE OF FIBER

And lentils, which boast the same healthful nutritional profile as beans, cook so quickly they can be made in about the same amount of time as rice. Serve these satisfying legumes with a simple roast chicken or panfried turkey sausages.

white beans with tomatoes & basil

Put onion in a fine-mesh strainer and rinse under cold running water. Drain well. Put beans in a colander, drain, rinse well, and drain again.

Cut tomatoes in half crosswise (or lengthwise, if they are Romas). Gently squeeze them and remove seeds and pulp with your finger, then chop. You should have about 1½ cups.

In a bowl, mix beans, tomatoes, vinegar, oil, basil, and onion. Season to taste with salt and pepper. Serve at once or chill for up to 4 hours.

4 SERVINGS • IRON-RICH • SOURCE OF VITAMINS

red onion, ¼ cup finely chopped

cannellini or other white beans, 2 cans (14 ½ oz each)

tomatoes, 2

balsamic vinegar, 2 Tbsp

extra-virgin olive oil, 1 Tbsp

fresh basil leaves, 3 Tbsp torn

salt and freshly ground pepper

sautéed spiced chickpeas

Heat oil in a large frying pan over medium-high heat. Add onion and garlic and cook until onion is wilted, reducing heat as necessary to prevent scorching, 4–5 minutes. Stir in spices and ½ tsp salt. Add chickpeas and lemon juice and cook, stirring, until chickpeas are heated through and well coated with spice mixture, 2–3 minutes.

4 SERVINGS • SOURCE OF MINERALS • CHOLESTEROL-BUSTER

olive oil, 2 Tbsp

yellow onion, ½, minced

garlic, 1 clove, minced

ground cumin, 1 tsp

ground coriander, ½ tsp

ground cinnamon, ¼ tsp

paprika, ¼ tsp

salt

chickpeas, 2 cans (14 ½ oz each), rinsed and drained

lemon juice, 2 Tbsp

Nearly raw chickpeas are the key to the toothsome texture of these savory Middle Eastern patties. Tuck the falafel into warmed pita bread rounds along with a leaf of red leaf lettuce, a spoonful of chopped tomatoes, a drizzle of plain yogurt or a dollop of tahini, and a sprinkling of mint. Keep the cooked falafel warm in a low oven while you finish panfrying the rest.

panfried falafel
with cumin & garlic

Bring a large pot of lightly salted water to a boil. Add chickpeas and cook until slightly softened but still very firm in the center, about 10 minutes. Drain chickpeas and cool slightly.

In a food processor, combine chickpeas with onion, garlic, and parsley and process until coarsely puréed. Transfer mixture to a bowl and stir in baking powder, cumin, 3/4 tsp salt, and red pepper flakes. Chill mixture until cold, about 1 hour.

Pour about 1 Tbsp oil into a large nonstick frying over medium-high heat. With wet hands, shape 1/4-cup portions of chickpea mixture into patties about 3 inches across. Place 3 or 4 patties at a time in the pan and cook, turning once, until browned on both sides, 4–6 minutes total. Repeat to shape and cook remaining falafel, adding more oil to pan as needed. Serve.

12–14 PATTIES, 4 SERVINGS • CHOLESTEROL-BUSTER • SOURCE OF LEAN PROTEIN

dried chickpeas, 1 1/2 cups

onion, 1, chopped

garlic, 3 cloves, chopped

fresh parsley leaves, 1 cup packed

baking powder, 1 tsp

ground cumin, 1 tsp

salt

red pepper flakes, 1/2 tsp

olive oil, 3 Tbsp

Socca, tasty crêpes made from chickpea flour, are a Provençal street food, cooked quickly on a sizzling griddle and eaten on the go. This version, which browns under the broiler, is something between a sturdy crêpe and a soft flatbread. The chickpea flour gives it a tender, almost custardlike texture. Serve it warm from the oven as a light lunch or as an appetizer.

niçoise socca
with olives, peppers & anchovies

chickpea flour, 1 2/3 cups

olive oil, 3 Tbsp

salt and freshly ground pepper

niçoise olives, 12, pitted

roasted red bell peppers, 1/4 cup, cut into strips

anchovy fillets, 8–12, rinsed and patted dry

In a large bowl, whisk together chickpea flour, 2 cups water, oil, and 3/4 tsp salt until smooth. Let stand at room temperature for 30 minutes. Put a heavy-duty 10-by-16-inch rimmed baking sheet or jellyroll pan in the oven and preheat to 500°F.

Remove pan from oven and grease with olive oil. Working quickly, pour batter into pan, tilting pan if necessary to evenly cover with batter. Arrange olives, bell pepper strips, and anchovy fillets evenly over surface of batter.

Switch oven setting to broil and place pan under broiler about 5 inches from heat source. Cook until batter is set and browned to lightly charred in spots, about 3 minutes. Remove pan from broiler and run a wide spatula under crêpe to release it from pan. Slide crêpe onto a cutting board. Sprinkle with pepper, cut into squares, and serve at once.

4 SERVINGS • SOURCE OF MINERALS • SOURCE OF GOOD FATS

Fattoush is an eastern Mediterranean salad traditionally made with coarsely chopped garden vegetables, a tart lemon dressing, and large croutons made of toasted or fried pita bread. With the addition of cooked turkey, this fresh salad becomes a vibrant warm-weather main dish.

turkey fattoush salad
with pita croutons

Preheat oven to 375°F. With your fingers, separate each pita into 2 rounds.

Brush one side of each pita round lightly with oil (using about 1 Tbsp total) and sprinkle lightly with paprika and salt. Arrange in a single layer on 2 large baking sheets and bake until crisp, 10–12 minutes. When cool enough to handle, break each round into 4 or 5 pieces.

In a large bowl, whisk together lemon juice, ⅛ tsp pepper, remaining 4 Tbsp olive oil, and ¼ tsp salt. Add lettuce, turkey, cucumbers, tomatoes, parsley, and pita pieces to bowl and toss to coat. Serve at once.

4 SERVINGS • SOURCE OF VITAMINS • SOURCE OF LEAN PROTEIN

whole-wheat pita bread rounds, 4

extra-virgin olive oil, 5 Tbsp

paprika, ¼ tsp

salt and freshly ground pepper

lemon juice, ¼ cup

red leaf lettuce, ½ head, torn into bite-sized pieces

cooked turkey, 1 lb, shredded or cut into pieces

English or Persian cucumbers, 1 cup seeded and chopped

ripe tomatoes, 1 cup seeded and chopped

parsley leaves, 3 Tbsp chopped

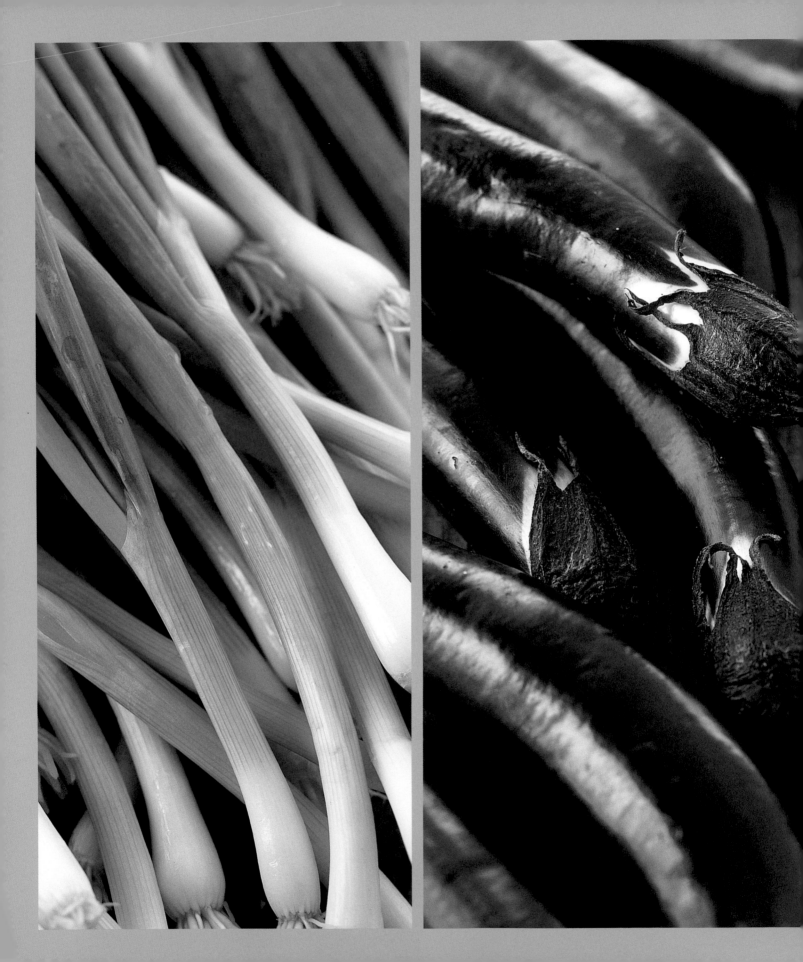

asian tonight

Some of the most vibrant, flavorful dishes in the world come from Asia and the subcontinent. China, Thailand, Vietnam, and India have influenced world cooking by inspiring the use of a free hand with fresh herbs, spices, garlic, ginger, and other aromatic and pungent seasonings. Moderate in the use of saturated fat and with a focus on carefully and lovingly prepared health-enhancing ingredients like fresh vegetables and soy, all the varied cuisines of Asia offer a great inspiration for eating well. Scout out a source for flavorful Asian pantry staples like rice vinegar, toasted sesame oil, Thai red curry paste, Madras curry powder, miso, coconut milk, and red chile paste. With these items on hand, you'll be able to throw together mouthwatering meals like Savory Eggplant Hot Pot, spicy Black Cod with Cashew Sambal, satisfying Stir-Fried Asparagus with Shiitakes & Sesame Seeds, and fragrant Golden Potatoes & Cauliflower with Curry & Fennel Seeds in no time.

These fresh vegetable rolls are tender bundles of rice noodles, lettuce, shredded carrots, and herbs. Arrange a platter of the ingredients and let diners make their own rolls, or assemble all of the rolls up to 30 minutes ahead of serving. Hold them at room temperature, covered well with plastic wrap.

summer vegetable rolls
with rice noodles

shiitake mushrooms, ½ lb

canola or peanut oil, 2 tsp

garlic, 1 clove, minced

soy sauce, 1 tsp plus more
for serving

thin dried rice noodles, 7 oz

rice-paper wrappers, 12–16

red bell pepper, 1, seeded and
thinly sliced

avocados, 2, pitted, peeled,
and sliced

butter lettuce, 1 head, torn
into bite-sized pieces

carrots, 2, peeled and julienned

**mixed fresh herb sprigs, such
as mint, cilantro, and basil,**
1 cup loosely packed

Asian red chile sauce, for serving

Asian peanut sauce, for serving

Trim stems from shiitakes and slice caps. Heat 1½ tsp oil in a large nonstick frying pan over medium-high heat. Add garlic and cook, stirring, until fragrant but not browned, about 30 seconds. Add mushrooms and sauté until they have released their juices, 3–4 minutes. Add 1 tsp soy sauce and cook until dry, about 1 minute longer. Transfer to a bowl and set aside.

Bring a pot of water to a boil. Add noodles, stir to separate, and cook until tender, 3–5 minutes. Drain and rinse under cold water. Toss with ½ tsp oil.

Fill a large, shallow bowl with very hot tap water. Soak rice-paper wrappers 1 or 2 at a time until flexible, about 30 seconds. Shake off excess water and stack on a plate. Place one wrapper flat on a work surface. Arrange a combination of noodles, bell pepper, avocado, mushrooms, lettuce, carrots, and herbs across center of wrapper; fold ends in over filling, then roll up tightly from edge closest to you. Repeat to make more rolls. Cut rolls in half and serve with a bowl of soy sauce with a dab of chile sauce and a bowl of peanut sauce alongside, for dipping.

4 STARTER SERVINGS • SOURCE OF VITAMINS • SOURCE OF ANTIOXIDANTS

Flank steak is easier to slice for stir-frying if you chill it in the freezer for about 30 minutes. To speed things up, you can also buy precut stir-fry meat, available at some butcher counters. Serve this quick and hearty stir-fry with wide rice noodles or steamed brown rice, if you like.

stir-fried beef & bok choy
with ginger

In a small bowl, mix sherry, soy sauce, and chile paste; set aside. Trim stem ends from baby bok choy and separate into leaves.

Heat ½ Tbsp oil in a wok or a large nonstick frying pan over high heat. When oil is hot, add bok choy and cook, stirring, just until crisp-tender, about 2 minutes. Transfer to a bowl.

Add remaining ½ Tbsp oil to pan. When hot, add garlic and ginger and cook, stirring, until fragrant but not browned, 15–30 seconds. Add beef to pan and cook, stirring, just until no longer pink, about 2 minutes.

Return bok choy to pan along with sherry mixture and cook for 1 minute until heated through. Serve at once.

4 SERVINGS • SOURCE OF VITAMINS • IRON-RICH

dry sherry, 2 Tbsp

soy sauce, 1 Tbsp

Asian red chile paste, ½ tsp

baby bok choy, 1 lb

peanut oil, 1 Tbsp

garlic, 2 cloves, minced

fresh ginger, 1 Tbsp minced or grated

flank steak, 1 lb, thinly sliced across the grain

nuts & peanuts

Hands down, nuts are one of the most nutritious foods you can eat. They're also one of the most well studied by scientists. Chock-full of heart-healthy fats, protein, and fiber, nuts play a well-documented role in good nutrition and prevention of disease. Eating an ounce of nuts several times a week has been linked with increased immunity and a significantly lower risk of heart disease and diabetes.

These nutrient-rich, flavorful little packages of monounsaturated fats and antioxidants have a lot to offer. Almonds are an excellent source of calcium. Peanuts, which are botanically considered legumes rather than nuts, are loaded with fiber and folate. Walnuts are a significant source of omega-3s, which boost the immune system and promote heart health. Cashews are lower in fat than most other nuts, and the fat they do contain is the same heart-healthy kind found in olive oil.

Because of their fat content, nuts of all types are uniquely satisfying, and their rich flavor enhances all kinds of dishes, including stir-fries and curries. Sprinkle toasted nuts onto your salads or pasta dishes, add them to your morning cereal, or simply enjoy them out of hand.

stir-fried chicken
with walnuts & basil

In a small bowl, mix soy sauce, lime juice, and honey; set aside. Core and seed bell pepper and thinly slice; set aside. Thinly slice chicken breasts across the grain and set aside.

Heat ½ Tbsp oil in a wok over high heat. Add bell pepper and cook just until wilted, 1–2 minutes. Transfer bell pepper to a plate and add ½ Tbsp oil to pan. Add shallots and cook, stirring constantly, until shallots begin to brown, 30 seconds–1 minute. Add chicken and cook, stirring frequently, until opaque, 3–4 minutes. Return bell pepper to pan and stir in soy sauce mixture, basil, and walnuts. Cook just until basil is wilted, about 1 minute. Serve with rice.

4 SERVINGS • SOURCE OF GOOD FATS • SOURCE OF LEAN PROTEIN

soy sauce, 3 Tbsp

lime juice, 2 Tbsp

honey, 2 Tbsp

red bell pepper, 1

boneless, skinless chicken breast halves, 3 (6 oz each)

peanut oil, 1 Tbsp

shallots, ½ cup thinly sliced

basil leaves, ½ cup torn

toasted walnut pieces, ½ cup

steamed brown rice, for serving

black cod
with cashew sambal

In a food processor, combine chiles, cashews, shallots, garlic, dried shrimp, and ½ tsp salt. Process to a paste, scraping down sides of bowl as needed. Heat ½ Tbsp oil in a large nonstick frying pan over medium-high heat. Scrape chile mixture into pan, reduce heat to medium, and stir frequently until mixture is aromatic and a few shades darker, 3–4 minutes. Whisk in coconut milk, lime juice, and brown sugar until well blended, and simmer for 1 minute. Transfer sauce to a bowl and wipe out pan with a paper towel.

Heat remaining ½ Tbsp oil over medium-high heat. Add fish and cook, turning once, until browned on both sides and opaque in center, about 6 minutes total. Transfer to plates and spoon sauce over fish. Serve.

4 SERVINGS • SOURCE OF GOOD FATS • SOURCE OF LEAN PROTEIN

red jalapeño or Fresno chiles, 5 or 6, seeded and chopped

toasted cashews, ½ cup

shallots, ¼ cup sliced

garlic, 3 cloves

Asian dried shrimp, ½ Tbsp minced

salt

peanut oil, 1 Tbsp

light coconut milk, 1 cup

lime juice, 5 Tbsp

brown sugar, ¼ cup packed

black cod fillets, 4 (6 oz each)

Thai red curry paste is a blend of fiery chiles, lemongrass, kaffir lime leaf, and galangal. A jarred version is an easy way to add a burst of complex flavor to quick dishes like this one. If you want something milder, reduce the curry paste by half. Serve with Jasmine Rice, page 210, if desired.

savory eggplant hot pot
with pork

pork tenderloin, 1 lb

salt

slender eggplants, 1 lb

red Fresno chiles, 2

canola oil, 1 Tbsp

Thai red curry paste, 2 tsp

chicken broth, 2 cups

lime juice, 3–3½ tsp

Asian fish sauce, 1–1½ tsp

cilantro sprigs, ¼ cup

Trim fat and any silvery membrane from tenderloin and cut into 1-inch chunks; sprinkle with salt. Trim ends from eggplants and cut into 1½-inch chunks. Slice chiles into rings and discard seeds.

Heat oil in a large saucepan over medium-high heat. Add curry paste and cook, stirring to break it up, until slightly toasted, 2–3 minutes. Add pork and cook, stirring frequently, until browned, 4–7 minutes. Transfer pork to a bowl and set aside.

Add eggplants, broth, and chiles to saucepan. Bring to a simmer and cook, stirring frequently, until eggplant is just tender, about 5 minutes. Return pork to pan along with any accumulated juices and simmer until pork is cooked through, 4–5 minutes longer. Stir in lime juice and fish sauce to taste. Garnish with cilantro sprigs and serve.

4 SERVINGS • SOURCE OF ANTIOXIDANTS • SOURCE OF FIBER

For a quick version of a cooling *raita* to spoon over this mildly spicy side dish, mix a cup of low-fat or nonfat yogurt with ½ cup grated cucumber and season it to taste with lemon juice, paprika, and salt. Try pairing this side dish with Chicken Kebabs with Tandoori Spices, page 112.

golden potatoes & cauliflower
with curry & fennel seeds

Cut potatoes into ¾-inch chunks. Remove leaves and core from cauliflower head and cut cauliflower into ¾-inch pieces.

Heat oil in a large, deep frying pan over medium heat. Add fennel seeds and cook until fragrant, about 30 seconds. Add onion and ¾ tsp salt and cook, stirring frequently and reducing heat as necessary to prevent scorching, until onion is soft and starting to brown, 7–10 minutes. Stir in garlic and chiles and cook for 1 minute. Stir in curry powder and cumin and cook for 1 minute longer.

Add potatoes, cauliflower, and 1½ cups water and bring to a boil over high heat. Reduce heat, cover, and simmer, stirring occasionally, until vegetables are tender when pierced, 15–20 minutes. Increase heat and cook, uncovered, until any remaining liquid is cooked away. Stir in parsley, if using, and serve.

4 SERVINGS • SOURCE OF VITAMINS • SOURCE OF ANTIOXIDANTS

unpeeled Yukon gold or other thin-skinned potatoes, 1¼ lb, scrubbed

cauliflower, 1 small head

olive oil, 2 Tbsp

fennel seeds, ½ tsp

onion, 1, halved and thinly sliced

salt

garlic, 2 cloves, minced

serrano chiles, 1–2, seeded and minced

Madras curry powder, 2 Tbsp

ground cumin, 1 tsp

fresh parsley leaves, ¼ cup chopped (optional)

The flavoring ideas given here are completely flexible. Try any of them with any type of rice. Whether short- or long-grain, the best rice you can choose is the whole-grain form, brown rice, which lowers cholesterol levels and protects the heart.

4 WAYS WITH rice

jasmine rice with cilantro & fried shallots

jasmine rice, 1 cup
peanut oil, 1 Tbsp
shallots, ½ cup thinly sliced
salt
cilantro, 1 Tbsp chopped

In a medium saucepan, bring 2 cups water to a boil. Add rice and reduce heat to very low. Cover and cook, without lifting lid, until liquid is absorbed and rice is tender, about 20 minutes.

While rice is cooking, heat oil in a nonstick frying pan over medium-high heat. Add shallots and ¼ tsp salt and cook, stirring, until browned, about 5 minutes. Remove from heat and set aside.

When rice is done, remove from heat and fold in shallots and cilantro. Serve.

4 SERVINGS • SOURCE OF FIBER • SOURCE OF MINERALS

sesame & soy brown rice

short-grain brown rice, 1 cup
soy sauce, 2 tsp
toasted sesame oil, 1 tsp
sesame seeds, 1 tsp toasted
seaweed sprinkles, 2 tsp
(see page 273)

In a medium saucepan, bring 2 cups water to a boil. Add rice, stir, and reduce heat to very low. Cover and cook, without lifting lid, until liquid is absorbed and rice is tender, 45–50 minutes.

Remove rice from heat and toss with soy sauce, sesame oil, sesame seeds, and seaweed sprinkles. Serve.

4 SERVINGS • SOURCE OF FIBER • SOURCE OF GOOD FATS

sticky rice with shiitakes & carrots

Rinse rice well under cold running water. Put rice in a bowl with water to cover and soak for 30 minutes. (This gives the rice a fluffy, sticky texture.)

In a medium saucepan, bring 1½ cups water to a boil. Drain rice and add to pan. Reduce heat to very low, cover, and simmer until rice is tender and water is absorbed, 15–18 minutes. Let stand, covered, for 5 minutes.

Heat oil in a nonstick frying pan over medium-high heat. Add shiitakes and cook, stirring frequently, until they begin to brown, 2–3 minutes. Stir in carrots and soy sauce and cook for 1 minute longer. Remove from heat.

In a small bowl, mix rice vinegar with sugar. Uncover rice and gently stir in the shiitake and rice vinegar mixtures. Serve.

4 SERVINGS • SOURCE OF VITAMINS • SOURCE OF MINERALS

short-grain white rice or sushi rice, 1 cup

peanut oil, 1 tsp

shiitake mushroom caps, ¾ cup diced

carrots, ¼ cup shredded

soy sauce, 1½ tsp

rice vinegar, 3 Tbsp

sugar, 1 tsp

basmati rice with coconut

Preheat oven to 350°F. Shake saffron in a dry frying pan over medium heat until fragrant and a shade darker, about 1 minute. Cool and crumble.

In a medium saucepan, bring 2 cups water to a boil. Add rice and saffron, stir, and reduce heat to very low. Cover and cook, without lifting lid, until liquid is absorbed and rice is tender, about 20 minutes.

Place shredded coconut on a baking sheet and toast in oven until lightly browned, 5–6 minutes.

Remove rice from heat and toss with coconut, currants, and orange zest. Serve at once.

4 SERVINGS • SOURCE OF FIBER • SOURCE OF MINERALS

saffron threads, ⅛ tsp

basmati rice, 1 cup

unsweetened shredded coconut, 3 Tbsp

currants, 2 Tbsp

orange zest, ¾ tsp chopped

This quick dish pairs tender spring asparagus with meaty shiitake mushrooms for a filling and satisfying vegetable stir-fry. Sesame seeds—especially the black variety—lend a savory flavor and subtle crunch to countless Asian dishes, but they are also densely nutritious and offer a surprising array of health benefits, due in part to their omega-3 fats.

stir-fried asparagus
with shiitakes & sesame seeds

asparagus, 1 lb

peanut oil, 3 Tbsp

garlic, 1 clove, minced

fresh ginger, 1 Tbsp minced or grated

shiitake mushrooms, 6 oz, stemmed and thinly sliced

dry white wine or sake, ¼ cup

chicken broth, ¼ cup

soy sauce, 1½ Tbsp

white and/or black sesame seeds, 2 tsp

To prepare asparagus, remove tough stem ends and cut spears diagonally into 2-inch pieces.

Heat oil in a large frying pan over high heat. Add garlic and ginger and cook, stirring frequently, until fragrant but not browned, about 30 seconds. Add mushrooms and cook, stirring frequently, until mushrooms begin to brown, about 2 minutes. Add asparagus and cook, stirring constantly, until bright green and crisp-tender, about 3 minutes. Add wine, broth, and soy sauce and cook until liquid is reduced and vegetables are tender, 2–3 minutes longer. Stir in sesame seeds. Serve.

4–6 SERVINGS • SOURCE OF VITAMINS • SOURCE OF MINERALS

Toss this colorful salad thoroughly before serving, so that the crunchy shreds of cabbage are well coated with the tangy dressing. Lime juice, fish sauce, and a little sugar give it a sweet-sour-salty kick. For a shortcut, use preshredded cabbage, available in the salad section of the supermarket.

shrimp & cabbage slaw
with chile sauce & lime

In a large bowl, mix fish sauce, vinegar, lime juice, sugar, and chile paste until sugar is dissolved and mixture is well blended.

Slice shrimp in half lengthwise and add to dressing along with both colors of cabbage, cilantro, and peanuts. Mix well, let stand 5 minutes, then mix well again. Serve at once.

4 SERVINGS • SOURCE OF ANTIOXIDANTS • SOURCE OF FIBER

Asian fish sauce, 3 Tbsp

rice vinegar, 3 Tbsp

lime juice, 3 Tbsp

sugar, 2 Tbsp

Asian red chile paste, 1 tsp

cooked shelled medium shrimp, 1 lb

red cabbage, 4 cups finely shredded

green or savoy cabbage, 4 cups finely shredded

cilantro leaves, 3/4 cup chopped

unsalted roasted peanuts, 1/2 cup chopped

broccoli

There's nothing fancy about broccoli. It's a humble, everyday workhorse of a vegetable, with a distinctive flavor that adapts well to a wide variety of seasonings. But broccoli's unassuming profile in the produce bin belies the fact that it is one of the most nutritious foods you can eat. Impressively high in vitamins, minerals, and fiber, providing substantial doses of antioxidants and phytochemicals, broccoli is also high in folate, a nutrient that is associated with the prevention of birth defects and diseases.

A member of the nutritious cruciferous family of vegetables, which includes other stars like cabbage, cauliflower, Brussels sprouts, and kale, broccoli is generally available year-round, but its peak season is during the cool months from late autumn to early spring.

From Europe to Asia, broccoli is a favorite in many culinary traditions. The bright green flowered crowns hold sauces well, and the stems are sweet and tender when cooked. Enjoy broccoli raw with dips or sliced in salads; steamed or gently boiled and lightly dressed; stir-fried, simmered in soups, tossed with pasta, or roasted to make a warm salad.

stir-fried broccoli
with black bean sauce

Rinse, drain, and mince black beans; set aside.

Heat oil in a large frying pan over medium-high heat. Add garlic and ginger and cook, stirring, until fragrant but not browned, about 30 seconds. Add broccoli and stir to coat with oil; cook for 1 minute. Add broth, black beans, and soy sauce, increase heat to high, and cook, stirring occasionally, until broccoli is tender and liquid is slightly reduced, 3–5 minutes. Serve at once.

4 SERVINGS • SOURCE OF VITAMINS • SOURCE OF MINERALS

Chinese salted black beans, 2 Tbsp

peanut oil, 1 Tbsp

garlic, 2 cloves, minced

fresh ginger, 1 Tbsp minced

broccoli, 1½ lb, cut into 1½-inch florets

chicken broth, ¾ cup

soy sauce, 1½ Tbsp

crisp-tender broccoli
with sesame dressing

In a large bowl, mix sesame oil, soy sauce, miso, lemon juice, and sugar until well blended.

Bring a large pot of lightly salted water to a boil. Add broccoli and cook just until crisp-tender, about 2 minutes. Drain well. Add broccoli to sesame-oil mixture and toss well to coat. Sprinkle with sesame seeds and serve.

4 SERVINGS • SOURCE OF ANTIOXIDANTS • SOURCE OF FIBER

toasted sesame oil, 1 Tbsp

soy sauce, 1 Tbsp

miso, 1 tsp

lemon juice, 2 tsp

sugar, 1 tsp

salt

broccoli, 1½ lb, cut into 2-inch florets

sesame seeds, 2 tsp, toasted

This simple, slightly spicy noodle dish is infinitely adaptable to whatever combination of vegetables you have on hand. Tahini, a paste made from toasted sesame seeds, is available in specialty foods stores and Middle Eastern markets. Use natural peanut butter without added sweeteners. If the oil has separated from the peanut butter, stir it in before measuring.

sesame noodles
with peanut sauce

carrots, 2, peeled

snow peas, ¼ lb, trimmed

whole-wheat spaghetti, ½ lb, broken in half

toasted sesame oil, 1 tsp

creamy peanut butter, 2½ Tbsp

soy sauce, 3 Tbsp

lime juice, 3½ Tbsp

tahini, 2 tsp

Asian red chile paste, 1½ tsp

cooked shelled shrimp, 1 lb

cilantro, ½ cup chopped

toasted peanuts, ¼ cup chopped

Slice carrots diagonally into ovals ⅛ inch thick, then cut each oval lengthwise into matchsticks.

Bring a large pot of lightly salted water to a boil. Add snow peas and cook just until crisp-tender, about 1 minute. Remove with a strainer and add carrots to the pot. Cook until just crisp-tender, about 2 minutes. Remove with a strainer and set aside.

Add spaghetti to boiling water and cook until al dente, 8–9 minutes or according to package directions. Reserve ¼ cup cooking water and drain noodles. Return noodles to pot and toss with sesame oil.

In a small bowl, mix peanut butter, soy sauce, lime juice, tahini, chile paste, and reserved pasta cooking water. Add to pasta along with cooked shrimp, vegetables, and cilantro and mix well. Garnish with peanuts and serve.

4 SERVINGS • SOURCE OF GOOD FATS • WHOLE GRAIN

california cuisine tonight

With its sunny climate and rich soil, California has an unrivaled wealth of fresh ingredients. Add to this the culinary influences of immigrants from every corner of the world, innovative chefs, plus a strong interest in eating seasonal and locally grown foods, and it's easy to see how California drew on the best other cuisines had to offer and developed a characterful, healthful cuisine all its own. The influence of California's renowned wine regions appears here in dishes like Seared Duck Breast with Zinfandel-Braised Red Cabbage. The fresh artisanal cheeses of California are showcased in dishes like Beet & Watercress Salad with Fresh Mozzarella and Tomato-Zucchini Tart with Goat Cheese. And the innovative spirit and casual, relaxed style of California's cooking come through in dishes like Rustic Flatbread with Egg, Arugula & Pecorino and Fish Tacos with Cabbage Slaw & Avocado Crema.

This simple, fresh-tasting asparagus soup is paired with hearty crab crostini, which are updated versions of open-faced crab melts. Choose slender stalks of asparagus for this dish. Sweeter and less fibrous than the thick ones, they will produce a lovely, silky soup when puréed.

asparagus soup
with crab crostini

asparagus, 2 lb

olive oil, 1 Tbsp

spring onions or sweet onion, 1 cup thinly sliced

chicken or vegetable broth, 3 ½ cups

salt and freshly ground pepper

cooked fresh lump or drained canned crabmeat, ¾ lb

green onion, 3 Tbsp minced

lemon juice, 1 Tbsp

mayonnaise, 2 Tbsp

Dijon mustard, ½ tsp

orange juice, ¼ cup

artisan-style sourdough bread, 8 slices (½ inch thick)

pecorino or dry jack cheese, 1 cup grated

To prepare asparagus, remove tough stem ends and cut into 1-inch pieces.

Heat oil in a large saucepan over medium heat. Add spring onions and cook, stirring frequently and reducing heat as necessary to prevent browning, until onions are soft and wilted, about 5 minutes. Add broth, asparagus, and ½ tsp salt. Simmer, uncovered, until asparagus is tender, about 15 minutes.

Meanwhile, in a bowl, mix crab, green onion, lemon juice, mayonnaise, and mustard. Season well with salt and pepper to taste.

In a blender or food processor, purée soup, in batches if necessary, until smooth. Return soup to pan and stir in orange juice and salt to taste.

Preheat broiler. Place bread slices on a baking sheet and toast one side under broiler. Turn bread slices over and top evenly with crab mixture. Sprinkle evenly with cheese and broil just until cheese is melted.

Ladle soup into 4 bowls and serve each with 2 crostini.

4 SERVINGS • SOURCE OF VITAMINS • SOURCE OF LEAN PROTEIN

A simple mixture of summer vegetables and fresh goat cheese bakes in a buttery cornmeal crust. Look for stone-ground cornmeal, which retains more of the nutritious (and flavorful) germ and bran than corn ground by metal grinders. Serve thin slices of this tart for a beautiful appetizer, or accompany it with a salad for a light lunch.

tomato-zucchini tart
with goat cheese

Heat oil in a large frying pan over medium-high heat. Add zucchini and sprinkle lightly with salt and pepper. Reduce heat and cook, stirring frequently, until zucchini is softened but not browned, about 5 minutes. Transfer zucchini to a paper towel–lined plate and allow to drain.

Position a rack in lower third of oven and preheat to 375°F. Roll dough out into a 12-inch circle about ¼ inch thick. Fit into a 9-inch fluted tart pan with removable sides. Fold edges of dough over and press into sides of pan, forming a double thickness around pan rim. Trim off any excess dough overhanging rim with a sharp paring knife.

Arrange half of goat cheese over bottom of crust. Arrange tomatoes and zucchini in overlapping concentric circles on top of goat cheese. Sprinkle lightly with salt and pepper and top with remaining goat cheese and sprigs of thyme.

Bake until crust is golden brown and juices are bubbling, 35–40 minutes. Remove pan rim and cool for 10 minutes. Cut into wedges and serve warm.

6–8 SERVINGS • SOURCE OF VITAMINS • WHOLE GRAIN

olive oil, 1 Tbsp

zucchini, ½ lb, sliced into ⅛-inch-thick rounds

salt and freshly ground pepper

Cornmeal Dough (page 268)

fresh goat cheese, 5 oz, crumbled

Roma tomatoes, ¾ lb, sliced

fresh thyme sprigs, 1 tsp coarsely torn

Lean and juicy Muscovy duck yields more meat than other domestic duck breeds. Much of its fat is rendered during searing, which turns the skin deliciously crisp. Zinfandel's big, ripe flavors work well for braising red cabbage, turning it soft, sweet, and mellow. Other full-bodied red wines, such as syrah (shiraz) or merlot can also be used.

seared duck breast
with zinfandel-braised red cabbage

boneless Muscovy duck breast halves, 4, trimmed of excess fat

salt and freshly ground pepper

red onion, ½, thinly sliced

zinfandel, 2 cups

red cabbage, 1¾ lb, thinly sliced

balsamic vinegar, 3 Tbsp

brown sugar, 1 Tbsp firmly packed

coriander seeds, 1 tsp

Sprinkle duck breasts with salt and pepper. Heat a large frying pan over high heat until hot. Add breasts, skin side down, and cook without turning until well browned, pouring off fat as needed, 5–8 minutes. Transfer to a baking sheet, skin side up, and set aside.

Pour off all but about 1 Tbsp fat and reduce heat to medium. Add onion and ½ tsp salt and cook, stirring frequently, until onion is soft, 8–10 minutes. Add wine, cabbage, vinegar, sugar, coriander, and several grindings of pepper. Bring to a simmer. Cover and simmer gently over medium-low heat, stirring occasionally, until cabbage is tender, about 1 hour.

About 40 minutes before cabbage is done, preheat oven to 400°F. Roast duck until a thermometer inserted into the thickest part registers 130°F for medium-rare, 15–18 minutes. Remove from oven and cover with foil; let stand for 10 minutes before slicing.

Season cabbage to taste with additional salt and pepper. Slice duck, removing skin if desired, and serve with cabbage.

4 SERVINGS • SOURCE OF VITAMINS • SOURCE OF ANTIOXIDANTS

new world grains

Everyone's talking about whole grains these days, which has led to the rediscovery of some neglected ancient pseudograins, or seeds, whose nutritional profile makes them exciting alternatives to wheat and other familiar grains. Quinoa and amaranth are complete proteins, a rarity in the plant world. They were both staple crops for the ancient peoples of South America, and after many years of being relegated to the dusty shelves of California health food stores, their popularity is spreading from the West Coast across the country.

Iron-rich quinoa, a crop native to the Andes, also supplies fiber, phosphorus, and magnesium in addition to protein. Cooked quinoa has a mild flavor and a light, fluffy texture, which makes it an interesting substitute for rice.

Amaranth, used as a staple crop by the Aztecs, has a similar nutritional profile. It contains iron, protein, and fiber, as well as magnesium and zinc.

Try your local natural foods market or check online for other sources of these and other less-common grains. You'll be rewarded with an interesting variety of flavors, textures, and nutrients.

seeded amaranth crackers
with sea salt & paprika

Preheat oven to 375°F. Line a baking sheet with parchment. In a food processor, blend flours, ½ tsp salt, and baking powder. Add 2 Tbsp oil and pulse until mixture resembles crumbs. Slowly add ¼ cup water and pulse just until dough comes together. Scrape out onto a well-floured board and use a well-floured rolling pin to roll out a rectangle ⅛ inch thick. Cut into squares. Place on baking sheet. Brush with oil, sprinkle with seeds, paprika, ½ tsp salt, and cheese. Bake until golden brown on edges and bottoms, 10–15 minutes. Cool and store in an airtight container for up to 3 days.

3 DOZEN CRACKERS • WHOLE GRAIN • SOURCE OF FIBER

all-purpose flour, ⅔ cup
amaranth flour, ⅓ cup
coarse sea salt
baking powder, ½ tsp
olive oil, 2 ½ Tbsp
poppy, fennel, sesame, and amaranth seeds, ¼ tsp each
paprika, ½ tsp
Parmesan cheese, 2 Tbsp grated

quinoa & radicchio salad
with dried cherries & pistachios

Put quinoa in a fine-mesh strainer and rinse well under cold water. In a medium saucepan, bring 2 cups of water to a boil. Add quinoa and reduce heat to low. Cover and simmer until grains are tender and water is absorbed, about 15 minutes. Fluff with a fork and transfer to a large bowl.

Core and thinly slice radicchio. Stir radicchio, vinegar, oil, cherries, pistachios, and parsley into warm quinoa. Season to taste with salt and pepper. Serve warm or at room temperature.

4 SERVINGS • WHOLE GRAIN • SOURCE OF VITAMINS

quinoa, 1 cup
radicchio, ½ head (about 4 oz)
balsamic vinegar, ¼ cup
olive oil, 2 Tbsp
dried tart cherries, ¼ cup
pistachios, ¼ cup chopped
fresh parsley, 3 Tbsp chopped
salt and freshly ground pepper

Confronting a whole artichoke might feel like laying siege to a fortress, but it's worth the effort, since this forbidding vegetable is not only delicious but also rich in antioxidants and vitamin C. Here, artichokes are filled with a savory mixture of oil-packed tuna and garlicky sourdough crumbs.

baked artichokes
with tuna & sourdough bread crumbs

Drain tuna, reserving 2 Tbsp oil. Reserve ¼ cup bread crumbs. In a bowl, mix remaining crumbs with tuna, reserved tuna oil, Parmesan, 2 Tbsp lemon juice, dill, ¼ tsp salt, and ¼ tsp pepper.

Bring a pot of salted water to a boil and add remaining 4 Tbsp lemon juice. Cut about 1 inch off the top of each artichoke, then snip off any remaining thorny tips with shears. Break off tough outer leaves, and use a vegetable peeler to peel stems. Trim off stem ends. Put artichokes in pot and cook until bases are tender when pierced with a knife, about 20 minutes. Remove with tongs and set aside, upside down, to drain and cool.

Preheat oven to 400°F. When cool enough to handle, scoop out prickly chokes from centers. Cut off stems, chop, and stir into tuna mixture. Spread leaves of each artichoke slightly, like a flower, and place upright in a baking dish. Spoon tuna mixture evenly into artichoke centers and top evenly with reserved bread crumbs. Bake, uncovered, until bread crumbs are golden brown, 15–20 minutes. Serve hot or warm.

4 SERVINGS • SOURCE OF VITAMINS • SOURCE OF OMEGA-3S

oil-packed tuna, 2 cans (6 oz each)
Garlic Bread Crumbs (page 268)
Parmesan cheese, ½ cup grated
lemon juice, 6 Tbsp
fresh dill, 1½ Tbsp chopped
salt and freshly ground pepper
large artichokes, 4

Flatbread for dinner is an easy proposition if you mix up the dough in the morning and let it rise in the refrigerator all day. Serve these crisp flatbreads topped with soft-set eggs one at a time, straight from the oven, accompanied with a simple green salad—or, if serving for brunch, a side of fresh fruit.

rustic flatbread
with egg, arugula & pecorino

olive oil, 1½ Tbsp

cornmeal, 2 Tbsp

Yeast Dough, at room temperature (page 269)

pecorino or Parmesan cheese, ⅔ cup grated

roasted red bell peppers, ¼ cup, cut into strips

large eggs, 8

salt and freshly ground pepper

sherry vinegar or red wine vinegar, 2 tsp

baby arugula leaves, 1 cup

frisée lettuce leaves, 1 cup bite-sized pieces

Preheat oven to 450°F. Lightly oil two 12-by-15-inch baking sheets and sprinkle with cornmeal.

Scrape yeast dough onto a lightly floured work surface and press gently to expel any air. Divide dough in half. Cover with a clean kitchen towel and let rest for 10 minutes. Roll or stretch one portion of dough into a 13-by-7-inch oval about ⅛ inch thick and place on a prepared baking sheet. Repeat with remaining dough and baking sheet. Brush each oval with ½ Tbsp olive oil and sprinkle each with half the cheese and bell pepper strips.

Bake flatbreads for 8 minutes. Remove from oven and crack 4 eggs onto each oval. Sprinkle eggs lightly with salt and pepper. Return flatbreads to oven, switching the positions of the baking sheets, and bake until crusts are well browned, 5–8 minutes longer.

In a large bowl, whisk remaining ½ Tbsp olive oil with vinegar. Add arugula and frisée and toss to coat. Slide each flatbread onto a cutting board and pile greens on top, dividing evenly. Cut into wedges and serve.

4–6 SERVINGS • SOURCE OF VITAMINS • SOURCE OF ANTIOXIDANTS

Tossed with buttery avocado and juicy ruby grapefruit, mâche—also known as lamb's lettuce—makes a sweet bed for lean and meaty seared tuna. Long foraged and cultivated in France, mâche is growing in popularity in the States, thanks to the efforts of California producers and chefs. It may look dainty, but it surpasses spinach in iron content.

seared tuna
with mâche, avocado & grapefruit salad

With a sharp paring knife, cut peel and pith from grapefruit, following curve of fruit. Holding grapefruit over a bowl to catch juices, use knife to cut individual segments of fruit from membrane. Put grapefruit segments in bowl along with juices.

Sprinkle tuna lightly with salt and pepper. Heat 1 Tbsp oil in a large nonstick frying pan over medium-high heat. Add tuna and cook until browned on first side, 2–3 minutes. Turn and brown second side, 4–5 minutes longer. The exterior of each piece should be browned, but tuna should remain raw in center. Transfer to a plate and let stand for 10 minutes.

Halve and pit avocados. Scoop flesh from peel and cut into 1-inch chunks. In a large bowl, mix vinegar, chile, and remaining 1 Tbsp olive oil. Add grapefruit segments and their juices, mâche, and avocado and mix gently.

Cut each piece of tuna crosswise into thin slices. Mound salad on individual plates and arrange tuna in overlapping slices on top. Serve.

4 SERVINGS • SOURCE OF ANTIOXIDANTS • SOURCE OF OMEGA-3S

regular or ruby grapefruit, 2

sushi-grade ahi tuna steaks, 4
(1 inch thick and 5 oz each)

salt and freshly ground pepper

olive oil, 2 Tbsp

ripe avocados, 2

rice vinegar, 2 Tbsp

serrano chile, 1, seeded and minced

mâche or butter lettuce leaves, 4 cups (about 4 oz) bite-sized pieces

For a delicious variation on this salad, check your local cheese shop or specialty foods market for *burrata,* a fresh mozzarella cheese filled with cream and fresh cheese curd. Its meltingly tender, creamy texture is delicious with the sweet beets and bitter watercress in this salad. Use two colors of beets if you like, or even striped Chioggia beets, if they are available.

beet & watercress salad
with fresh mozzarella

baby red and/or golden beets, 1½–1¾ lb

extra-virgin olive oil, 3 Tbsp

champagne vinegar, 2 Tbsp

fresh orange juice, 2 Tbsp

orange zest, 1 tsp grated

salt and freshly ground pepper

watercress, ¼ lb, cut into bite-sized sprigs

fresh mozzarella cheese, 1 lb, cut into wedges

Preheat oven to 400°F. Trim root and stem ends from beets and rinse well. Wrap beets in heavy-duty foil, making a separate packet for each color, and bake until beets can be pierced easily with a knife, 45 minutes–1 hour. Unwrap and cool. Gently peel beets with a paring knife, cut into quarters, and put in a small bowl.

In a large bowl, whisk together oil, vinegar, orange juice, zest, and ½ tsp salt. Pour half of this mixture over beets and stir to coat. Add watercress to remaining dressing in large bowl and toss to coat.

Mound watercress on individual plates or on one large platter and top with beets. Arrange cheese around beets and drizzle with any vinaigrette left over from dressing watercress. Sprinkle with a few grindings of pepper and serve at once.

4 SERVINGS • SOURCE OF VITAMINS • CALCIUM-RICH

Enthusiasts disagree about what makes the ultimate fish taco, but in its simplest form, this iconic dish consists of tender pieces of fish, a little dressed cabbage, and a creamy dressing folded into a warm tortilla. *Crema* is a Mexican-style cultured cream similar to sour cream. Yogurt makes a good substitute, blending with avocado into a creamy sauce.

fish tacos
with cabbage slaw & avocado crema

Halve and pit avocado and scoop flesh into a food processor. Add *crema*, 2 tsp lime juice, ¾ tsp cumin, and ¼ tsp salt. Blend just until smooth. Transfer *crema* to a bowl, cover, and refrigerate for up to 2 days.

To make slaw, in a large bowl, combine cabbage, cucumber, bell pepper, remaining 2 Tbsp lime juice, 1 Tbsp olive oil, chile, cilantro, onion, remaining ½ tsp cumin, and ¼ tsp salt. Mix well. Cover and refrigerate for 1–6 hours.

Heat a grill to high, and oil rack. Place fish on a plate and coat lightly with remaining ½ Tbsp oil. Sprinkle both sides lightly with salt and pepper. Grill fish, carefully turning once with a wide spatula, until opaque in center, 6–8 minutes total. Transfer fish to a platter, break into 8 pieces, and cover loosely with foil. Wrap tortillas in foil and warm on grill, about 5 minutes.

To assemble tacos, place 2 tortillas on a serving plate and top with a piece of fish. Stir cabbage slaw well and top each piece of fish with about ¼ cup slaw and 2 Tbsp *crema*. Repeat to assemble remaining tacos. Serve at once.

4 SERVINGS • SOURCE OF FIBER • SOURCE OF OMEGA-3S

ripe avocado, 1

***crema* or plain low-fat or nonfat yogurt,** 1 cup

lime juice, 2 Tbsp plus 2 tsp

ground cumin, 1¼ tsp

salt and freshly ground pepper

savoy cabbage or green leaf lettuce, 2 cups shredded

English cucumber, ½ cup diced

red bell pepper, ½ cup diced

extra-virgin olive oil, 1½ Tbsp

serrano chile, 1, seeded and minced

cilantro, 3 Tbsp chopped

onion, 2 Tbsp minced

halibut or other firm-fleshed white fish fillet, 1 lb, skin removed

corn tortillas, 8

desserts

Eating well for dessert is easy when you consider that some of the tastiest foods are good for you, too. Dark chocolate, with its disease-fighting plant compounds called polyphenols, adds luxurious richness to Chocolate-Banana Bonbons and is the main ingredient in Dark Chocolate Bark with Toasted Almonds & Dried Blueberries. Fresh berries bursting with vitamins meld with tart, antioxidant-rich lemon in creamy Pudding Cakes and combine with heart-healthy red wine and naturally low-fat fresh ricotta in the stunning Berries in Sangria Syrup. You will find delectable surprises in this chapter, such as tender fig- and date-filled Buttery Dried-Fruit Bars, refreshing Honey & Cardamom Frozen Yogurt, and sweet, rich Kabocha Cupcakes made with puréed winter squash. You'll also find a handful of crisp recipes, easily adaptable to whatever fresh fruit is in season, so that every meal can end with a taste of something wholesome yet sweet.

This refreshing frozen yogurt has a subtle flavor that goes wonderfully well with fresh or baked summer fruit. Try a scoop with Apricot-Cherry Crisp, page 261, or Baked Nectarines with Cinnamon-Almond Streusel, page 262. For the creamiest texture, eat this frozen yogurt within a day or two of making it.

honey & cardamom
frozen yogurt

whole or low-fat milk, ½ cup

sugar, ½ cup

cardamom pods, 2 tsp, coarsely chopped

plain whole-milk yogurt, 3½ cups

honey, ½ cup

vanilla extract, 1 Tbsp

lemon juice, 2 tsp

In a small saucepan over medium heat, stir milk, sugar, and cardamom pods together until sugar is dissolved and mixture comes to a boil. Cover and let stand at room temperature until cool, about 30 minutes. Strain into a large bowl, discarding cardamom pods.

Whisk yogurt, honey, vanilla, and lemon juice into milk mixture. Freeze in an ice-cream maker according to manufacturer's instructions.

Serve at once, or transfer frozen yogurt to an airtight container and freeze until firm, about 4 hours.

ABOUT 1 QUART • LIVE CULTURE • CALCIUM-RICH

These sweet, fiber-rich fruit bars are delicious eaten slightly warm with frozen yogurt, but they also make a wholesome lunch box treat. You can make the dough a week ahead and store it in the refrigerator, but the filling is easiest to spread the day it is made. Look for very moist dried figs and dates.

buttery dried-fruit bars
with figs & dates

Combine figs and dates in a heatproof bowl. In a small saucepan over medium heat, stir ¼ cup water, 2 Tbsp brown sugar, and lemon juice until mixture comes to a boil. Pour over fruit, cover bowl, and let stand until cool, about 1 hour. In a food processor, purée mixture, including any unabsorbed liquid, until smooth. Scrape into a bowl, cover, and set aside.

Using a mixer, beat butter and remaining ½ cup plus 2 Tbsp brown sugar until smooth. Beat in egg and vanilla. In another bowl, stir together flours, baking powder, and salt. Stir flour mixture into butter mixture, blending well. Divide dough and wrap each half in plastic. Refrigerate for 1 hour.

Preheat oven to 375°F. Butter an 8-inch square baking pan. On a floured board, roll one portion of dough just larger than pan, about ¼ inch thick, and trim with a knife into an 8-inch square. Fit into pan and spread fruit evenly over dough. Roll out and trim remaining piece of dough in the same way and place over fruit. Bake until golden brown on top, 20–25 minutes. Run a knife around inside edge of pan, cool completely, then invert onto a cutting board. Trim a thin strip from edges, then cut into 16 bars.

16 BARS • WHOLE GRAIN • SOURCE OF FIBER

dried mission figs, 8 oz, stemmed and coarsely chopped

pitted dates, 4 oz (about ½ cup), chopped

brown sugar, ¾ cup firmly packed

lemon juice, 1 Tbsp

unsalted butter, ½ cup, softened

large egg, 1

vanilla extract, 1 tsp

all-purpose flour, 1¼ cups

whole-wheat flour, ½ cup

baking powder, 1 tsp

salt, ¼ tsp

Naturally sweet and creamy when frozen, bananas are full of potassium. Cover them with dark chocolate and nuts and you have a quick, healthy treat. For this recipe, choose bright yellow bananas that are not too ripe and freckled but rather still have some firmness.

chocolate-banana bonbons
with toasted almonds

semisweet chocolate, 12 oz, chopped

toasted almonds or pecans, 2/3 cup chopped

bananas, 2

In a bowl set over a pan of barely simmering water, melt chocolate, stirring occasionally, until smooth. Remove pan from heat, but leave bowl of chocolate on top of pan to keep warm.

Place nuts in a shallow bowl. Line a baking sheet with waxed paper.

Peel bananas and cut into 1/2-inch rounds. Drop 1 banana slice at a time into chocolate and turn to coat. Lift out with a fork, tapping fork gently on bowl edge to allow excess chocolate to drip back into bowl. Place banana slice on baking sheet and sprinkle with nuts. Repeat to dip and coat remaining banana slices.

Freeze bonbons until chocolate is set, about 20 minutes, then transfer to an airtight container and store in the freezer for up to 1 week.

ABOUT 30 BONBONS, 8 SERVINGS • SOURCE OF ANTIOXIDANTS

berries

Let color be your guide when shopping for berries. Their bright jewel hues of red, purple, and blue signal their powerful antioxidant punch. Blueberries are the leader in antioxidant capacity, but most berries are good sources of these and other phytochemicals—plant compounds linked with a strong immune system and good health—as well as vitamins and minerals. Naturally sweet, berries are a delicious way to add more nutrition to your menu.

In summer, fresh berries need little augmentation to become a delicious meal or snack. Choose ripe blackberries, raspberries, blueberries, and strawberries at the farmers' market or produce stand and eat them as soon as you can; fresh berries are delicate and perishable. Add a handful to your hot or cold breakfast cereal, sprinkle them over frozen yogurt, toss them in a spinach salad with fresh goat cheese, or cook them up into a satisfying dessert. In fall and winter, look for cranberries and huckleberries, which make delicious pies and crisps. The year-round availability of good-quality frozen berries means that these sweet superfoods are available anytime for breakfast smoothies and after-dinner fruit crisps.

berries in sangria syrup
with ricotta cream

With a paring knife, cut two 2- to 3-inch strips of zest from orange. Using fine rasps of a handheld grater, remove another 1 tsp zest and set aside.

Combine wine, ½ cup sugar, and zest strips in a small saucepan over medium heat, stirring until sugar dissolves. Boil until liquid is reduced to about 1 cup, 10–15 minutes. Cool, remove zest, and pour over berries.

In a food processor, combine ricotta, liqueur, vanilla, grated zest, and remaining 2 Tbsp sugar and process until smooth. Spoon berries and syrup into goblets and top with a dollop of ricotta mixture. Serve at once.

4 SERVINGS • SOURCE OF ANTIOXIDANTS • CALCIUM-RICH

large orange, 1
dry red wine, 1½ cups
sugar, ½ cup plus 2 Tbsp
mixed raspberries, blueberries, and/or blackberries, 2 cups
part-skim ricotta cheese, 8 oz
Grand Marnier, 1 Tbsp
vanilla extract, ¼ tsp

pudding cakes
with mixed berries

Preheat oven to 350°F. Divide berries among four 8-oz ramekins. Place ramekins in a baking pan with at least 1 inch of space all around them.

In a large bowl, beat egg yolks with vanilla and sugar until thick and creamy. Whisk in flour, lemon juice, butter, and milk until smooth and thin. With a mixer on high speed, beat egg whites with cream of tartar until soft peaks form. Gently fold egg whites into yolk mixture.

Divide batter evenly among ramekins. Place pan on pulled out center rack of oven and pour hot water into pan to a depth of 1 inch. Bake until tops of cakes spring back when lightly touched in the center, about 30 minutes. Remove ramekins and let stand for 5 minutes before serving warm.

4 SERVINGS • SOURCE OF ANTIOXIDANTS • SOURCE OF VITAMINS

mixed raspberries, blueberries, and/or blackberries, 1½ cups
large eggs, 2, separated
vanilla extract, 2 tsp
sugar, ½ cup
all-purpose flour, ¼ cup
lemon juice, ¼ cup
unsalted butter, 2 Tbsp, melted
low-fat milk, 1 cup
cream of tartar, 1 pinch

This moist yet sturdy little cake, accompanied by juicy ripe strawberries macerated in sugar and citrus zest, is just right for dessert, breakfast, or tea. Hearty whole-grain polenta gives the tea cake an appealing bright golden color as well as a pleasantly rustic texture.

polenta tea cake
with citrus-sugared strawberries

In a food processor, pulse ¼ cup granulated sugar and 1 tsp each lemon and orange zest until blended. Transfer to a bowl and set aside.

Preheat oven to 350°F. Butter and flour a 6-cup tube pan. With a mixer on medium-high speed, beat butter and remaining 1 cup granulated sugar until smooth. Add eggs one at a time, beating well after each addition. Beat in almond extract and remaining 1 tsp lemon zest.

In a small bowl, stir together flour, polenta, baking powder, and salt. Stir half of flour mixture into butter mixture. Stir in buttermilk, followed by remaining flour mixture. Scrape batter into prepared pan and bake until a tester inserted into center of cake comes out clean, 40–50 minutes.

Cool cake in pan for 10 minutes, then invert onto a cooling rack. Remove pan and cool cake completely.

An hour before serving, hull and slice strawberries and stir in reserved citrus sugar. When ready to serve, dust cake with confectioners' sugar if desired, slice cake, and spoon strawberries alongside or on top of cake slices.

8 SERVINGS • WHOLE GRAIN • SOURCE OF ANTIOXIDANTS

granulated sugar, 1¼ cups

lemon zest, 2 tsp grated

orange zest, 1 tsp grated

unsalted butter, ¾ cup, softened

large eggs, 2

almond extract, 1 tsp

all-purpose flour, 1¼ cups

stone-ground polenta, ¼ cup

baking powder, 1 tsp

salt, ¼ tsp

buttermilk, ¾ cup

confectioners' sugar, for garnish (optional)

ripe strawberries, 2 pint baskets

Kabocha squash, also known as Japanese pumpkin, has a dense, sweet flesh that is perfect for these tender cupcakes, which can be eaten as is, dusted with confectioners' sugar, or spread with the frosting given in the recipe. You can bake and mash the squash up to 2 days ahead. Any extra purée will keep well in the freezer for up to 6 months.

kabocha cupcakes
with vanilla cream cheese frosting

kabocha squash, 1 (about 2 lb)

canola oil, ½ cup

granulated sugar, 1 cup

large eggs, 2

vanilla extract, 1 Tbsp

all-purpose flour, 1½ cups

baking soda, 1 tsp

ground cinnamon, ½ tsp

ground cloves, ¼ tsp

salt, ¼ tsp

low-fat milk, ¼ cup

Neufchâtel cheese, 8 oz, at room temperature

confectioners' sugar, 1 cup

vanilla extract, 2 tsp

lemon juice, 1 tsp

Preheat oven to 350°F. Cut squash in half crosswise and place, cut side down, in a baking pan with ¼ cup water. Bake until very soft when pressed, 45 minutes–1 hour. Cool, then scoop out and discard seeds. Scrape flesh from peel. Mash with a fork or purée until smooth; measure out 1 cup.

Line a cupcake pan with 12 paper liners. In a large bowl, whisk together oil, granulated sugar, eggs, vanilla, and 1 cup mashed squash until smooth. In a small bowl, stir together flour, baking soda, cinnamon, cloves, and salt. Stir flour mixture into squash mixture, followed by milk, until well blended. Spoon batter into pan, filling each cup about ⅔ full.

Bake until a tester inserted in the center of a cupcake comes out clean, 18–20 minutes. Remove cupcakes from pan and cool completely on a rack.

To make frosting, with a mixer on high speed, beat cheese with confectioners' sugar, vanilla, and lemon juice until smooth. Spread frosting on cooled cupcakes and serve at once, or refrigerate frosted cupcakes for up to 1 day.

12 CUPCAKES • SOURCE OF ANTIOXIDANTS • CALCIUM-RICH

Get a hit of brain-boosting antioxidants and omega-3s at dessert time with this nutty, fruity chocolate bark. Melting the chocolate slowly over very low heat will yield the best results. You can also melt it a few seconds at a time in a microwave; stop cooking before the chocolate is completely melted and stir out the last few lumps until smooth.

dark chocolate bark
with toasted almonds & dried blueberries

Line a baking sheet with waxed paper. In a bowl set over a pan of barely simmering water, melt chocolate, stirring occasionally, just until mixture is melted and smooth. Remove from heat.

Stir almonds and blueberries into chocolate. Using a heatproof rubber spatula, scrape mixture onto prepared baking sheet and spread out to a thickness of ¼ inch.

Chill chocolate bark until completely firm, about 2 hours. Break or cut into chunks. Store in an airtight container in refrigerator for up to 1 month.

12 OZ BARK, 4 SERVINGS • SOURCE OF ANTIOXIDANTS • SOURCE OF MINERALS

bittersweet chocolate, 8 oz, chopped

toasted almonds, ⅓ cup coarsely chopped

dried blueberries, ¼ cup

You can make extra batches of crisp topping and freeze them in individual zippered freezer bags for several months. That way, you're ready at a moment's notice to bake up a great fruit dessert. Serve with a drizzle of cream, if you like.

fruit crisps

crisp topping

rolled oats, 1 cup

all-purpose flour, ¾ cup

light brown sugar, ½ cup firmly packed

ground cinnamon, ¾ tsp

salt, ¼ tsp

unsalted butter, ½ cup, cut into pieces

walnuts, ⅓ cup chopped

Combine oats, flour, brown sugar, cinnamon, and salt. With a mixer fitted with paddle attachment on low speed, or using your fingers, mix or rub in butter until mixture forms coarse crumbs and begins to come together.

Stir in walnuts. Use at once, or seal in a zippered plastic freezer bag and freeze for up to 6 months. (Crumble frozen topping right over fruit without thawing it first, and expect to add a few minutes to the baking time.)

TOPPING FOR 1 CRISP • SOURCE OF FIBER • CHOLESTEROL-BUSTER

nectarine-blackberry filling

sugar, ¼ cup

cornstarch, 1 Tbsp

nectarines, 3 lb, halved, pitted, and sliced

blackberries, 1 cup

Crisp Topping (above)

Preheat oven to 375°F. In a large bowl, mix sugar and cornstarch. Add nectarines and blackberries and mix well. Pour fruit into a 9-inch square or round baking dish. Sprinkle evenly with topping mixture.

Bake until topping is golden brown and juices are bubbling, 50–60 minutes. Let crisp stand for at least 15 minutes before serving, and serve warm or at room temperature.

8 SERVINGS • SOURCE OF ANTIOXIDANTS • SOURCE OF VITAMINS

Nectarine-blackberry and apricot-cherry crisps make use of luscious midsummer fruit, while an apple-date crisp enlivens the table in midwinter. You may, of course, use any kind of seasonal fruit the market has to offer for this versatile dish.

apricot-cherry filling

Preheat oven to 375°F. In a large bowl, mix sugar and cornstarch. Add apricots and cherries and mix well. Pour fruit mixture into a 9-inch square or round baking dish. Sprinkle evenly with crisp topping.

Bake until topping is golden brown and juices are bubbling, about 1 hour. Let crisp stand for at least 15 minutes before serving, and serve warm or at room temperature.

8 SERVINGS • SOURCE OF VITAMINS • SOURCE OF ANTIOXIDANTS

sugar, ¼ cup

cornstarch, 1 Tbsp

apricots, 3 lb, pitted and quartered

sweet cherries, ½ lb, pitted

Crisp Topping (opposite, top)

apple-date filling

Preheat oven to 375°F. In a large bowl, mix sugar and cornstarch. Add apples, dates, and apple juice and mix well. Pour fruit into a 9-inch square or round baking dish. Sprinkle evenly with topping mixture.

Bake until topping is golden brown and apples are tender when pierced with a knife, 50–60 minutes. Let crisp stand for at least 15 minutes before serving, and serve warm or at room temperature.

8 SERVINGS • SOURCE OF VITAMINS • SOURCE OF FIBER

sugar, ¼ cup

cornstarch, 1 Tbsp

apples, 3 lb, peeled, cored, and sliced

dates, ½ cup pitted and chopped

apple juice, ¼ cup

Crisp Topping (opposite, top)

Warm baked summer fruit is irresistible when topped with a crumbly, buttery almond streusel topping. Substitute peaches or plums as you wish. For a delightful contrast in temperature, serve the warm nectarines with Honey & Cardamom Frozen Yogurt, page 246, or a drizzle of cold heavy cream.

baked nectarines
with cinnamon-almond streusel

unsalted butter, 3 Tbsp, cut in pieces

firm nectarines or peaches, 4

all-purpose flour, 6 Tbsp

brown sugar, 6 Tbsp firmly packed

ground cinnamon, ½ tsp

salt, ⅛ tsp

toasted almonds, ⅓ cup chopped

Preheat oven to 400°F. Lightly butter a 9-by-13-inch baking dish.

Cut nectarines in half and remove pits. Cut a thin slice off round side of each half and arrange pit side up in prepared dish.

In a bowl or a food processor, stir or whirl together flour, sugar, cinnamon, and salt. Cut in butter with a pastry cutter or two knives, or pulse in food processor until mixture resembles coarse crumbs. Stir in almonds. Squeeze streusel mixture into small handfuls and distribute it evenly over cut sides of nectarine halves, pressing it lightly to adhere.

Bake until nectarines are tender and streusel is browned, about 20 minutes. Serve fruit warm.

4 SERVINGS • SOURCE OF VITAMINS • SOURCE OF FIBER

Panna cotta, which means "cooked cream" in Italian, is an ethereal dessert that traditionally consists of cream and milk set very softly with gelatin. This enlightened version uses tangy yogurt in place of the cream. It's delicious on its own or accompanied with a sweet-tart winter fruit compote.

yogurt panna cotta
flecked with vanilla bean

In a small bowl, sprinkle gelatin over ½ cup milk. Let stand without stirring until gelatin is moistened, about 10 minutes.

Pour 1 cup milk into a small saucepan over medium heat. Scrape seeds from vanilla bean into milk, then add bean pod, ½ cup sugar, and zest. Stir until sugar is dissolved and mixture comes to a simmer. Remove from heat. Add gelatin mixture and stir until gelatin is completely dissolved, 3–5 minutes. Transfer to a large bowl. Cool until lukewarm, about 10 minutes, then remove vanilla bean and orange zest. Whisk in yogurt until well blended.

Lightly brush insides of six 6-oz ramekins or small bowls with oil and place on a rimmed baking sheet. Divide yogurt mixture evenly among prepared ramekins. Cover and refrigerate until set, 8 hours–2 days.

To serve, gently run a knife between panna cotta and sides of ramekins to loosen. Place a plate over each ramekin and, holding plate and ramekin together, invert and remove ramekin. If desired, spoon compote over each panna cotta, drizzling plate with its juice. Serve at once.

4 SERVINGS • CALCIUM-RICH

unflavored gelatin, 2 tsp
(one 1-oz envelope)

2% milk, 1½ cups

vanilla bean, 1, split lengthwise

sugar, ¾ cup

orange zest, 3 strips, each
2–3 inches long

plain whole-milk yogurt, 2 cups

vegetable oil, for ramekins

Cranberry-Orange Compote,
for serving (page 268; optional)

The hint of fresh tangerine juice in this refreshing granita, or ice, highlights the citrusy notes of Earl Grey tea, which is sometimes flavored with the essential oil of bergamot orange peel. If you grow bergamot orange in the garden, use its juice and zest here in place of the tangerine.

earl grey granita
with a tangerine twist

loose Earl Grey tea leaves, 6 Tbsp

sugar, ¾ cup

fresh tangerine or orange juice, ¼ cup

tangerine zest strips, 6

In a small saucepan, bring 4 cups water to a boil. Remove from heat and add tea leaves. Cover and let steep until tea is strong and dark but not bitter, 3–5 minutes. Strain tea into a large glass or stainless-steel bowl, discarding leaves, and whisk in sugar until dissolved. Chill until cold.

Whisk in tangerine juice and place bowl in freezer. Stir mixture about every hour, using a fork to break up ice crystals as they form, until mixture is granular and slushy, 4–6 hours. Cover and freeze for up to 1 day, or serve at once, spooning granita into tall glasses. Garnish with zest twists.

6 SERVINGS • SOURCE OF VITAMINS • SOURCE OF ANTIOXIDANTS

basic recipes

corn bread

fine stone-ground cornmeal, 1 ⅔ cups

all-purpose flour, 1 ⅔ cups

sugar, ½ cup

baking powder, 2 Tbsp

salt, 1 tsp

whole milk, ⅔ cup

large eggs, 4, lightly beaten

butter, ½ cup plus 2 ½ Tbsp, melted

Preheat the oven to 375°F. Grease a 9-inch round springform or square pan with melted butter.

In a large bowl, stir together the cornmeal, flour, sugar, baking powder, and salt. Make a well in the center of the mixture and pour in the milk, eggs, and melted butter. Stir together the wet and dry ingredients until they are just combined. Take care not to overmix; the batter should be slightly lumpy.

Pour the batter into the prepared pan. Bake until the corn bread is golden brown around the edges and on top, 25–30 minutes. A cake tester inserted into the center should come out clean.

Let the corn bread cool in the pan for about 15 minutes. If using a springform pan, release the sides of the pan to free the corn bread. If using a square pan, run a thin spatula around the edges of the corn bread to free it from the pan, then turn it out.

cornmeal dough

all-purpose flour, 1 cup

fine stone-ground cornmeal, ½ cup

salt, ½ tsp

unsalted butter, 6 Tbsp, cut into pieces

large egg, 1

In a food processor or large bowl, combine the flour, cornmeal, and salt. Add the butter and pulse or rub in with your fingers or a pastry blender until the mixture resembles coarse crumbs. Add the egg and ¼ cup cold water and pulse or stir just until the dough begins to come together. Flatten the dough into a disk, wrap it in a sheet of plastic, and chill it for at least 1 hour or up to 2 days.

cranberry-orange compote

oranges or tangelos, 2 ½ lb

sugar, ¼ cup

lemon juice, 1 Tbsp

pomegranate seeds, ¼ cup

With a sharp knife, cut the peel and pith from the oranges. Working over a bowl, cut between the membranes to release the orange segments and juices into the bowl. Combine the sugar, lemon juice, and ¼ cup water in a small saucepan. Bring to a boil. Remove the syrup from the heat and pour over the oranges. Chill, then stir in pomegranate seeds.

firm polenta

olive oil

stone-ground polenta, 2 cups

salt

Lightly grease a 9-by-13-inch baking dish with oil. In a large, heavy-bottomed pot, bring 8 cups water to a boil.

Pouring slowly and stirring constantly with a whisk, add the polenta and ½ tsp salt to the boiling water. Reduce the heat to medium-low and cook uncovered, stirring occasionally, until the mixture is thick and the texture is no longer grainy, about 25 minutes.

Pour the polenta into the prepared dish and chill until set, about 2 hours.

garlic bread crumbs

artisan-style sourdough bread, 2 slices (about 3 by 4 inches and ½ inch thick each)

garlic, 1 clove, peeled

Preheat the oven to 300°F. Place the bread slices on a baking sheet and bake them, turning once, until they are lightly toasted, about 15 minutes total. Rub one side of each slice of warm toast with the garlic clove. Cool, then tear the toasts into chunks. Put them in a food processor, in 2 batches if necessary, and process into coarse crumbs.

olive tapenade

kalamata olives, ½ cup pitted and chopped
garlic, 1 small clove
extra-virgin olive oil, 2 Tbsp
lemon juice, 2 tsp
orange zest, ½ tsp grated
freshly ground pepper

In a food processor, combine the olives and garlic and process until finely chopped. Add the oil, lemon juice, orange zest, and a few grindings of pepper and purée until well blended.

roasted poblanos

poblano chiles, 4
olive oil

Preheat the oven to 375°F. Rub the chiles with oil and roast on a rimmed baking sheet, turning occasionally, until blistered and soft, 30 minutes. Cool, then remove the skins, cores and seeds.

roasted tomatoes

tomatoes, 3 lb
olive oil, 1 Tbsp
balsamic vinegar, 2 Tbsp
garlic, 1 clove, minced
salt and freshly ground pepper
dried thyme, ½ tsp

Preheat the oven to 325°F. Slice the tomatoes in half and place, cut side up, on a baking sheet. Mix the oil, vinegar, garlic, ¼ tsp salt, ¼ tsp pepper, and the thyme. Spoon the mixture evenly over the tomatoes. Bake until the tomatoes are soft and wrinkled, about 1 hour.

salsa verde

anchovy fillets, 2
fresh parsley leaves, 1¾ cups
olive oil, 3 Tbsp
balsamic vinegar, 3 Tbsp
garlic, 1 clove
capers, 1 Tbsp, drained
mustard, 1 tsp

Rinse the anchovy fillets, pat them dry, and coarsely chop. In a food processor, combine the anchovies with the parsley, olive oil, vinegar, garlic, capers, and mustard. Process until coarsely puréed.

tomato sauce

extra virgin olive oil, 1 Tbsp
garlic, 1 clove, crushed
ripe plum tomatoes, 1½ lb, peeled and seeded, **or canned tomatoes with juice,** 2 cups
dry white wine or vermouth, 2 Tbsp
salt and freshly ground pepper
fresh basil, 1 Tbsp shredded

Heat the oil in a large frying pan over medium-high heat. Add the garlic and sauté until golden, 1–2 minutes. Add the tomatoes with their juices and crush them with a wooden spoon. Bring the mixture to a boil, then reduce heat to medium. Add the wine, ½ tsp salt, and a pinch of pepper and simmer for 15 minutes. Remove from the heat and let stand for 5 minutes. Discard the garlic. Purée in a food processor. Add the basil just before using.

yeast dough

active dry yeast, 1 tsp
warm water (110°F), ¾ cup
olive oil, 2 Tbsp
all-purpose flour, 2–2¼ cups
salt, ½ tsp

In a large bowl, sprinkle the yeast over the warm water and let stand until foamy, about 5 minutes. Stir in the olive oil. Gradually stir in 2 cups of the flour and the salt until a soft dough forms.

In a stand mixer fitted with a dough hook, beat the dough on high speed until it is soft and smooth and no longer feels sticky, beating in more flour 1 Tbsp at a time as needed to prevent sticking, 5–7 minutes. Transfer the dough to a clean bowl and cover with plastic wrap. Let the dough rise until doubled in volume, 35–45 minutes. Punch the dough down, cover, and refrigerate for at least 8 hours or up to overnight.

About 2 hours before serving, bring the dough to room temperature (this will take 45 minutes–1 hour).

glossary

ARUGULA Also known as rocket, this peppery salad green has notched leaves averaging 3 inches in length. It is a good source of vitamin A. Look for bunches with perky, bright green leaves.

ASIAN CHILE OIL Made by soaking chiles and seasonings in oil, chile oil is used throughout Asia to add heat to a dish. Look for it in bottles at Asian markets, online sources, and well-stocked supermarkets.

ASIAN DRIED SHRIMP Sun-dried shrimp are used in Chinese and Southeast Asian cuisines to add savory flavor to curries and other dishes. Look for them in Asian markets. Refrigerated, they will keep for several months.

ASIAN FISH SAUCE An amber-colored liquid made from salted and fermented fish, fish sauce is used in Asian cuisines for seasoning and adding depth of flavor. The longer the sauce is fermented, the more it develops a savory, but not particularly fishy, flavor. The Thai version, known as *nam pla,* is the most commonly available.

ASIAN PEANUT SAUCE Also known as satay sauce, this spicy, peanut butter–based sauce is used in Southeast and East Asia as a condiment and ingredient. Jarred versions are available in Asian markets, online sources, and well-stocked supermarkets.

ASIAN RED CHILE PASTE Versions of this concentrated blend of chiles and seasonings exist throughout Asia, but one of the most common is the Indonesian one, *sambal ulek.* Look for it at Asian markets or online sources.

ASIAN RED CHILE SAUCE Also known as sriracha, after a town in Thailand, this sauce is used throughout Asia and is nearly always found on the tables of Vietnamese restaurants. Use it as a condiment or dipping sauce.

BEANS, DRIED Nutritional powerhouses, dried beans are a beneficial source of complex carbohydrates, protein, and dietary fiber. They are also rich in vitamins, including the B vitamin folate, and are naturally low in fat, calories, and sodium. For convenience, canned beans may be used in most recipes. Rinse canned beans to remove added sodium.

black Small and uniformly black with a shiny surface. Used widely in Latin American cooking to make pot beans, soups, and dips.

borlotti This rosy beige bean with maroon speckles, used in Italian cooking, is similar to the cranberry bean (below) and is also available fresh.

cannellini This ivory-colored bean with a smooth texture is popular in salads, side dishes, and soups, including the classic Italian minestrone.

chickpea A large beige bean with a rich, nutty flavor and a firm texture, chickpeas are also known as garbanzos.

cranberry A mild-flavored bean with reddish flecks, cranberry beans' color fades when the beans are soaked and cooked. Also called Roman bean or borlotti bean. Sold fresh as well as dried.

green French lentils Varieties of this quick-cooking, disk-shaped legume include Le Puy, a small, dark green variety with a mild flavor.

pinto This pale brown bean has a spotty, mottled apprearance to its skin, which evens out during cooking. The full, earthy flavor of pinto beans is especially appreciated in the cuisine of the American Southwest.

white kidney Sometimes mistaken for cannellini, this mild-flavored bean is used often in Italian dishes and is a good substitute for cannellini in most recipes.

BRAN This outer covering of grains is removed during milling. Whole grains retain more of the bran than refined forms of a grain. Bran is a rich source of dietary fiber and other nutrients.

BROCCOLI RABE With its long, thin stalks and flowering heads, broccoli rabe has an assertive, bitter flavor. It contains many of the same nutrients as broccoli.

BROTH Whether a recipe calls for chicken, vegetable, or beef broth, the best choice for healthful cooking is a broth that is low in sodium. Reduced-sodium broths are widely available canned or in aseptic packaging. Sodium content can also be limited by preparing homemade stocks. These broths also give the cook more control over the seasoning of a dish.

BUTTER, UNSALTED Also labeled "sweet butter," unsalted butter is preferred by cooks who want a lower-salt alternative to regular salted butter. Some cooks prefer unsalted butter for its fresher, more pronounced flavor. Because the salt in butter acts as a preservative, unsalted butter in its original wrapping should be kept in the refrigerator for no longer than 6 weeks.

CHILES These pungent pepper pods are a good source of vitamin C (in green chiles) and vitamin A (in red chiles). They also are rich in beneficial antioxidants.

chipotle This is a jalapeño chile that has been dried and smoked. Chipotles are dark brown and very hot, with a smoky, slightly sweet flavor. They are widely available canned in a flavorful tomato-based sauce called *adobo*.

jalapeño This fleshy chile ranges in spiciness from slightly hot to fiery and measures 2–4 inches long. Green jalapeños are the most common form, but ripe red jalapeños are also available. Serrano chiles may be substituted.

poblano This shiny, dark green, bell pepper–shaped chile has a sharp, peppery flavor that mellows nicely when it is roasted.

serrano Slightly slimmer than a jalapeño and about 2 inches long, this chile has as much heat as a jalapeño and may be used in its place.

CHINESE SALTED BLACK BEANS Available in Asian markets, Chinese salted black beans, sometimes called fermented black beans, have a salty, pungent flavor that gives an earthy complexity to dishes such as stir-fries.

COCONUT MILK Made by soaking and pressing coconut flesh, coconut milk is available in regular and light versions. It is rich in calories and minerals. The light version has less fat and about a quarter of the calories of the regular version.

COTIJA CHEESE This firm and crumbly cow's milk cheese, named for its town of origin in Mexico, plays a role similar to Parmesan's in that country's cuisine.

FARRO One of the world's oldest grains, farro, also called emmer wheat, is high in protein and has a deliciously nutty, wheatlike flavor. Favored in Italy, it is used in soups and salads or cooked like risotto. Look for semi-pearled farro, which is partly hulled and cooks more quickly than whole-grain farro, but still retains some of the beneficial bran.

HARISSA This North African condiment is made of chiles, often smoked, and garlic; some spices may be added. Available in cans, jars, and tubes.

HOISIN SAUCE Hoisin sauce is a savory Chinese condiment made of fermented soybeans, sugar, chiles, and salt.

HOT-SMOKED SALMON Unlike cold smoked salmon, which is usually sold in thin slices, hot-smoked salmon is most often sold as a chunky piece of fillet. It has been smoked at temperatures high enough to fully cook the fish, which results in a firmer texture and more rounded flavor.

MISO Protein-rich miso paste is made of fermented soybeans combined with rice, barley, or wheat. The various types of miso are defined by the grain used. White miso, made with rice, is pale yellow and has a mild flavor. Its subtly sweet taste is appreciated in many Japanese seafood and vegetable dishes.

MUSHROOMS, DRIED Appreciated for their intense flavors and firm textures, dried mushrooms, after rehydrating, may be substituted for fresh in most cooked dishes, although they may need to cook longer to become tender.

porcini Porcini have a full, sweet fragrance and earthy flavor. Excellent in risottos and pasta sauces.

shiitake Dried shiitakes have a rich, meaty flavor and texture.

MUSHROOMS, FRESH Valued primarily for their rich, woodsy flavor, mushrooms are also rich in vital minerals, particularly selenium, as well B vitamins and heart-healthy fiber.

cremini Brown-capped mushroom that may be substituted for white button mushrooms. Cremini have a firmer texture and fuller flavor.

shiitake Buff to dark brown in color and meaty in texture, shiitakes are the most popular mushroom in Japan. Select shiitake mushrooms that have smooth, plump caps. The stems are quite tough and are not usually eaten.

white The all-purpose variety sold in grocery stores, white mushrooms are sometimes called button mushrooms. Look for fresh-looking specimens with tightly closed caps.

OILS Cooking oils, fats that are liquid at room temperature, play an essential role in the kitchen. A recipe's other ingredients and its heat requirements usually will suggest which oil is most appropriate to use.

canola Pressed from rapeseed, a relative of the mustard plant, canola is high in healthful monounsaturated fat.

This bland oil is recommended for general cooking and baking; however, it can smell unpleasant at the high temperatures required for frying.

olive Pressed from the fruit of the olive tree, this oil is high in monounsaturated fat. Extra-virgin olive oil is produced from the first press of the olives without the use of heat or chemicals. It has a clear green or brownish hue and a fruity, slightly peppery flavor.

peanut Pressed from peanuts, peanut oil has a slightly rich, nutty flavor in its unrefined version. It is often used in salad dressings and dipping sauces for a variety of Asian dishes. The refined version is useful for stir-frying at high temperatures.

safflower This flavorless oil is pressed from safflower seeds. It has a high smoke point, and is high in polyunsaturated fat.

toasted sesame This deep amber-colored oil is pressed from toasted sesame seeds. Use it sparingly to add a rich, nutty flavor to dishes.

PANKO Japanese bread crumbs, or *panko*, are made from wheat flour. The coarse flakes are used to coat foods before cooking, giving them a light, crunchy coating. Look for *panko* in Asian markets and well-stocked supermarkets.

PARSLEY This commonly used herb has a fresh flavor and high antioxidant activity. For best flavor, always choose flat-leaf or Italian parsley.

PRESERVED LEMONS Available in jars at markets that carry Middle Eastern ingredients, preserved lemons impart a unique salty-sour note to any dish they are used in. To replace preserved lemon, add 1 extra tablespoon lemon juice and ¼ teaspoon salt.

QUESO FRESCO Meaning "fresh cheese" in Spanish, *queso fresco* is a soft, tangy, lightly salted cow's milk cheese that is crumbled or sliced before it is added to dishes. Mild feta cheese may be substituted, but it should be rinsed first to remove excess salt.

RAS EL HANOUT This Moroccan spice blend gives stews and tagines a complex flavor. If you can't find it, substitute cumin and coriander in equal amounts.

RICE PAPER WRAPPERS Sometimes labeled *bánh tráng,* these thin, brittle sheets made from rice flour and water are sold in Asian markets.

SAFFRON THREADS The bright yellow-orange spice known as saffron is derived from the stigmas of a crocus flower. In higher-quality versions of the spice, the threadlike stigmas remain intact. Toasting saffron before crumbling it into a dish brings out the best flavor.

SALT The most basic and ancient of seasonings, salt comes in many forms, including table salt, sea salt, and kosher salt. Table salt usually contains added iodine to help prevent deficiencies. Sea salt, by contrast, rarely has additives, and contains more minerals than table salt. It is produced naturally by evaporation, with the taste of each variety reflecting the location where it was made. Available in coarse or fine grains that are shaped like hollow, flaky pyramids, sea salt adheres better to foods and dissolves more quickly than table salt. Many cooks prefer kosher salt, the type used in the recipes in this book. Its large, coarse flakes are easy to handle, and it usually contains no additives or preservatives. Kosher salt can be used more liberally since it does not taste as salty as regular table salt.

SCALLOPS The most common types of this plump saltwater mollusk are the sea scallop and the bay scallop. The former is about 1½ inches in diameter, while the latter is about ½ inch in diameter.

SEAWEED SPRINKLES Japanese seasoned seaweed sprinkles, or *furikake*, give flavor and crunch to nutty short-grain brown rice and other Asian dishes. Look for seaweed sprinkles in markets that carry Asian ingredients, and check the ingredient list, as some brands contain MSG.

SESAME SEEDS These tiny flat seeds range in color from white to tan to black and provide protein and polyunsaturated fat. Added to a recipe or sprinkled over a finished dish to contribute a nutty flavor and subtle texture, sesame seeds are widely used in Asian, African, Middle Eastern, and Latin American cuisines.

SMOKED PAPRIKA This Spanish spice, made from smoked paprika peppers, comes in sweet, semisweet, and hot versions. Use whichever suits your taste.

SOY SAUCE This ever-popular Asian seasoning is made from fermented soybean meal and wheat. Always choose reduced-sodium soy sauce: While still high in sodium, it has about half the sodium of regular soy sauce, with popular brands containing slightly more than 1,000 milligrams of sodium per tablespoon. In addition to being more healthful, the low-sodium version gives cooks more control over seasoning.

SPRING ONION Though their name is often used interchangeably with green onions or scallions, true spring onions are bulbing onions pulled before the bulb forms. They resemble small leeks.

TAHINI Tahini is a paste made of sesame seeds, used in Mediterranean and Middle Eastern cooking. It is one of the main ingredients in hummus. Look for it in Middle Eastern markets, online sources, and well-stocked supermarkets.

THAI BASIL A popular ingredient in Thai cooking, Thai basil's purple-tinged leaves are pointier than those of sweet basil, and their flavor is more biting.

THAI RED CURRY PASTE This fragrant, somewhat spicy mixture includes chiles, shallots, garlic, galangal, lemongrass, and kaffir lime zest. Look for it in the Asian foods aisle of the supermarket.

TOFU Mild-flavored, ivory-colored tofu, made from curdled soy milk, is rich in protein and easily digestible. Also known as bean curd, it comes in varying densities and is labeled "firm," "soft," or "silken." Sold in blocks packed in water or in aseptic packaging, tofu should be drained, rinsed, and then drained again before use. When storing tofu, change the water daily to help keep it fresh. Other forms of tofu, such as smoked, are also available. Tofu is often fortified with calcium. It is naturally low in calories and sodium, high in protein, and cholesterol free, making it a particularly healthy food choice.

TUNA, SUSHI-GRADE This very fresh and clean-tasting fish can be eaten raw. It may be labeled sushi- or sashimi-grade at fish markets. Tuna is a high-quality protein source rich in beneficial omega-3 fatty acids.

VINEGARS Made from a variety of red or white wines or, like cider vinegar and rice vinegar, from fruits and grains, vinegars can be further seasoned by infusing them with fresh herbs, fruit, garlic, or other flavorings. All offer a healthful, low-fat way to season a range of different foods.

nutritional analysis

The recipes in this cookbook have been analyzed for significant nutrients. Having these nutritional values at your fingertips will help you create balanced meals. As a basic guideline, a typical 2,000-calorie-a-day diet should include no more than 65 g of fat (of which only up to 20 g should be saturated fat); 300 mg of cholesterol; 2400 mg of sodium; 300 g of carbohydrate; 25 g of fiber; and 50 g of protein.

Keep in mind that the calculations reflect nutrients per serving. Not included are optional ingredients, or those that are suggested as an alternative in the recipe or recipe note. For recipes yielding a range of servings, the calculations are for the high end of that range. The analysis assumes the use of 2-percent milk unless specified otherwise in a recipe, and reduced-sodium broth and soy sauce.

The numbers for all nutritional values have been rounded using the guidelines for reporting nutrient levels on U.S. food labels. Many recipes in this book call for a specific amount of salt and also suggest seasoning to taste; however, if you are on a sodium-restricted diet, it is prudent to omit salt. If you have particular concerns about salt intake or other nutrient needs, consult a doctor or a registered dietitian.

page	breakfast	CALORIES kcal	PROTEIN gm	CARBS gm	TOT. FAT gm	SAT. FAT gm	CHOL mg	FIBER gm	SODIUM mg
18	maple-almond granola	350	8	48	15	1.5	0	6	60
21	breakfast panini	340	12	46	13	2.5	10	2	370
23	irish porridge	160	4	22	7	3.5	20	3	75
23	oatmeal with pumpkin & cinnamon	240	6	50	3	.5	0	5	70
24	shirred eggs	110	7	1	8	3.5	220	1	230
27	oatmeal scones	400	8	53	19	8.5	50	3	670
28	multigrain ricotta waffles	330	13	41	13	3	85	3	440
30	strawberry-banana smoothie	200	7	37	2	1	5	2	85
30	carrot-pineapple smoothie	180	8	31	2	1.5	10	3	105
31	blueberry-pomegranate smoothie	210	7	40	2.5	1.5	10	3	90
31	chocolate–peanut butter smoothie	260	12	34	10	3.5	10	4	160
33	root-vegetable hash	470	14	70	16	3	210	10	530
34	buckwheat pancakes	240	10	42	4	1.5	75	3	660
37	yogurt parfaits	250	8	37	9	4	20	4	75

page	big salads	CALORIES kcal	PROTEIN gm	CARBS gm	TOT. FAT gm	SAT. FAT gm	CHOL mg	FIBER gm	SODIUM mg
42	roasted sweet potato salad	660	10	130	12	1.5	0	18	230
45	seared scallops	240	20	14	10	1.5	35	3	740
46	warm spinach salad	330	9	22	21	6	25	10	500
49	black beans & avocado salad	320	25	22	13	2	150	11	370
49	avocado & crab salad	230	15	4	15	2	85	7	390
51	chicken & mango salad	700	40	51	37	7	105	5	250
52	watermelon & feta salad	330	29	24	13	6	200	2	630
55	chopped cucumber salad	240	9	10	19	9	50	1	770
55	pear & walnut salad	240	4	10	16	3	5	3	290
57	fava bean & corn salad	210	8	28	8	1	0	7	710

page	soup for all seasons	CALORIES kcal	PROTEIN gm	CARBS gm	TOT. FAT gm	SAT. FAT gm	CHOL mg	FIBER gm	SODIUM mg
62	savory barley soup	260	11	40	4	.5	0	7	360
65	spring vegetable soup	110	14	2	4	1.5	110	1	350
67	roasted tomato soup	130	6	11	5	.5	0	3	180
67	tomato & bread soup	210	9	23	8	1	0	4	320
68	sweet pea soup	220	14	19	10	2.5	5	6	350
71	chicken & wild rice soup	220	26	11	7	1.5	55	1	170
72	potato soup with kale & sausage	310	21	29	11	2.5	30	4	650
75	vegetable-lentil soup	210	17	17	6	1.5	5	6	690
77	chipotle tortilla soup	400	39	15	20	7	90	4	700
77	roasted red pepper soup	300	17	22	15	3.5	5	6	280
78	curried butternut squash soup	330	11	40	11	6	0	14	450
81	white bean & escarole soup	720	61	51	26	7	175	14	510

page	seafood for dinner	CALORIES kcal	PROTEIN gm	CARBS gm	TOT. FAT gm	SAT. FAT gm	CHOL mg	FIBER gm	SODIUM mg
86	panfried trout with corn bread salad	470	34	34	21	4	165	4	900
89	salmon burgers	490	30	29	27	5.5	60	2	800
90	braised halibut	400	37	35	11	1.5	45	5	430
92	salmon broiled with lemon	370	34	2	25	6	85	1	140
92	cod with honey-miso glaze	190	32	10	2	.5	75	0	430
93	grilled halibut with mango salsa	290	36	18	8	1	55	2	230
93	roasted bass with carrot purée	290	42	4	9	1.5	175	2	280
95	spice-rubbed snapper	210	35	2	6	1	65	0	170
96	beer-steamed mussels	150	15	7	4.5	.5	40	0	140
99	smoked salmon frittata	180	16	1	13	5	280	0	430
99	red curry salmon	630	36	3	52	12	85	1	550
101	fish & shellfish stew	370	48	18	9	1.5	160	2	500
102	steamed tilapia	220	36	3	5	1	65	<1	410

page	lean & mean	CALORIES kcal	PROTEIN gm	CARBS gm	TOT. FAT gm	SAT. FAT gm	CHOL mg	FIBER gm	SODIUM mg
108	pork tenderloin	370	33	19	9	2.5	90	3	135
111	turkey salad	220	22	8	9	2	55	2	680
112	chicken kebabs	330	56	5	7	2.5	150	2	430
115	pork medallions	390	34	4	26	4.5	90	2	330
116	chicken breasts with mustard sauce	400	33	34	12	2.5	75	2	510
116	chicken breasts with fig relish	250	27	10	10	2	75	2	135
117	chicken breasts & cherry tomatoes	230	28	5	10	2	75	1	140
117	chicken breasts with lemon & capers	230	27	2	10	2	75	0	190
118	grilled chicken with cilantro pesto	400	32	4	29	5	75	1	250
121	turkey lettuce wraps	380	41	3	21	5	120	<1	560
123	skirt steak salad	450	49	10	23	7	100	2	750
123	beef tenderloin with sautéed mushrooms	360	34	4	21	6	95	<1	210
124	grilled flank steak with baby artichokes	440	36	8	26	6	70	8	410

page	meatless meals	CALORIES kcal	PROTEIN gm	CARBS gm	TOT. FAT gm	SAT. FAT gm	CHOL mg	FIBER gm	SODIUM mg
130	couscous salad with dried fruit	430	9	48	22	2.5	0	4	330
133	buckwheat crêpes	470	15	56	20	9	190	17	680
134	spicy roasted cauliflower pasta	240	9	30	9	1.5	<5	6	500
137	pumpkin cassoulet	840	49	135	14	3	5	29	320
138	spicy three-bean chili	350	15	57	6	1	0	15	320
141	grilled tofu kebabs	150	9	4	11	1.5	0	<1	720
141	steamed tofu with greens	360	20	18	24	7	0	6	520
143	wild rice cakes	550	17	26	42	11	190	4	780
144	polenta lasagna	350	16	36	15	6	35	7	580
147	eggplant & golden squash tagine	360	14	42	13	1.5	0	15	380

page	farmers' market fresh	CALORIES kcal	PROTEIN gm	CARBS gm	TOT. FAT gm	SAT. FAT gm	CHOL mg	FIBER gm	SODIUM mg
152	sweet frites	390	5	63	8	1.5	<5	9	210
155	grilled cherry tomatoes	180	6	5	15	7	35	1	470
156	roasted broccoli	140	4	7	12	1.5	0	0	160
158	spicy broccoli rabe with garlic	40	1	2	2	.5	0	1	370
158	pan-steamed asian greens	40	2	2	3	.5	0	1	125
159	creamed chard with crème fraîche	150	4	6	12	4	10	3	640
159	turnip greens with bacon	130	4	7	8	1.5	10	5	340
161	roasted summer vegetables	300	10	14	21	6	15	9	530
162	grilled radicchio	80	1	3	7	1	0	<1	150
165	grilled squash & orzo salad	340	12	26	22	3.5	<5	7	570
165	baked acorn squash	200	3	32	5	.5	0	10	100
167	gratin of winter root vegetables	220	6	32	6	1.5	<5	7	400
168	sautéed brussels sprouts	110	4	7	7	1	0	4	300
171	marinated summer beans	190	8	8	13	3.5	15	5	220

page	mediterranean tonight	CALORIES kcal	PROTEIN gm	CARBS gm	TOT. FAT gm	SAT. FAT gm	CHOL mg	FIBER gm	SODIUM mg
176	barley risotto	390	40	20	14	4	70	4	520
179	spanish peperonata	90	1	6	6	1	0	3	220
180	mint tabbouleh	240	6	25	11	1.5	0	8	150
183	farro salad with artichoke hearts	290	8	26	16	1.5	0	7	350
183	bulgur & lentil pilaf	320	14	33	12	1.5	0	12	230
185	green lentil salad	200	6	20	10	1.5	0	5	630
186	quick-sautéed calamari	660	46	89	14	2.5	265	16	1020
188	lentils with garlic & herbs	120	5	11	7	1	0	4	180
188	beans with sage & pancetta	340	22	48	8	2	10	15	260
189	white beans with tomatoes & basil	340	19	56	5	1	0	22	75
189	sautéed spiced chickpeas	260	12	33	9	1.5	0	9	280
191	panfried falafel	220	7	22	12	1.5	0	6	540
192	niçoise socca	270	11	23	15	2	10	5	950
195	turkey fattoush salad	530	41	34	24	4.5	85	6	690

page	asian tonight	CALORIES kcal	PROTEIN gm	CARBS gm	TOT. FAT gm	SAT. FAT gm	CHOL mg	FIBER gm	SODIUM mg
200	summer vegetable rolls	470	9	48	25	2.5	0	14	1050
203	stir-fried beef & bok choy	320	32	2	15	5	70	1	320
205	stir-fried chicken with walnuts	510	28	61	17	2.5	55	6	500
205	black cod with cashew sambal	420	35	23	21	10	70	1	400
206	savory eggplant hot pot	280	37	4	10	2.5	90	4	490
209	golden potatoes & cauliflower	210	5	30	8	1	0	5	430
210	jasmine rice with cilantro & shallots	220	4	42	4	.5	0	1	140
210	sesame & soy brown rice	210	4	42	3	.5	0	3	100
211	sticky rice with shiitakes & carrots	250	4	52	2	.5	0	1	75
211	basmati rice with coconut	200	3	31	7	6	0	3	10
212	stir-fried asparagus	110	3	7	7	1.5	0	2	160
215	shrimp & cabbage slaw	300	31	16	11	1.5	220	5	1290
217	stir-fried broccoli with black bean sauce	80	6	8	4	.5	0	0	270
217	crisp-tender broccoli	80	4	4	5	.5	0	4	500
218	sesame noodles with peanut sauce	360	34	23	13	2.5	220	6	880

page	california cuisine tonight	CALORIES kcal	PROTEIN gm	CARBS gm	TOT. FAT gm	SAT. FAT gm	CHOL mg	FIBER gm	SODIUM mg
224	asparagus soup	510	46	41	17	5.5	80	7	1750
227	tomato-zucchini tart	250	7	20	16	9	60	2	280
228	seared duck breast with red cabbage	420	50	19	5	1	245	5	550
231	seeded amaranth crackers	100	2	10	5	1	0	<1	320
231	quinoa & radicchio salad	300	8	38	14	1.5	0	4	85
233	baked artichokes with tuna	320	35	17	10	3	25	8	800
234	rustic flatbread with egg	370	20	35	18	5	290	3	540
237	seared tuna with avocado & grapefruit salad	470	36	13	27	4.5	55	8	30
238	beet & watercress salad	430	22	17	30	13	70	3	940
241	fish tacos	420	32	31	18	3	40	8	360

page	desserts	CALORIES kcal	PROTEIN gm	CARBS gm	TOT. FAT gm	SAT. FAT gm	CHOL mg	FIBER gm	SODIUM mg
246	honey & cardamom frozen yogurt	200	4	38	4	2.5	15	0	55
249	buttery dried-fruit bars	410	5	66	14	8	59	5	150
250	chocolate-banana bonbons	310	4	29	18	8	0	3	0
253	berries in sangria syrup	320	8	39	5	3	20	4	75
253	pudding cakes with mixed berries	280	7	37	10	5	125	3	60
255	polenta tea cake	440	6	58	20	12	100	3	180
256	kabocha cupcakes	340	5	40	17	5	55	1	220
259	dark chocolate bark	370	5	38	22	10	0	3	5
260	nectarine-blackberry crisp	390	6	55	17	8	30	5	75
261	apricot-cherry crisp	400	6	56	17	8	30	6	75
261	apple-date crisp	420	4	64	16	8	30	5	75
262	baked nectarines	340	5	44	16	6	25	4	75
265	yogurt panna cotta	270	9	47	6	4	25	0	95
265	cranberry-orange compote	200	3	44	.5	0	0	6	5
266	earl grey granita	100	0	26	0	0	0	0	0

index

Oxmoor House®

Published by Oxmoor House
Oxmoor House books are distributed by Sunset Books
80 Willow Road, Menlo Park, CA 94025
Telephone: 650-321-3600 Fax: 650-324-1532

VP and Associate Publisher Jim Childs
Director of Marketing Sydney Webber

Oxmoor House and Sunset Books are divisions of
Southern Progress Corporation

WILLIAMS-SONOMA, INC.
Founder & Vice-Chairman Chuck Williams

EAT WELL
Conceived and produced by Weldon Owen Inc.
415 Jackson Street, San Francisco, CA 94111
Telephone: 415-291-0100 Fax: 415-291-8841

In Collaboration with Williams-Sonoma, Inc.
3250 Van Ness Avenue, San Francisco, CA 94109

A Weldon Owen Production
Copyright © 2008 Weldon Owen Inc.
and Williams-Sonoma, Inc.

First printed in 2008
10 9 8 7 6 5 4 3 2 1

ISBN-13: 978-0-8487-3270-7
ISBN-10: 0-8487-3270-7

Printed in China by SNP-Leefung.

WELDON OWEN INC.
Executive Chairman, Weldon Owen Group John Owen
CEO and President Terry Newell
Senior VP, International Sales Stuart Laurence
VP, Sales and New Business Development Amy Kaneko
Director of Finance Mark Perrigo

VP and Publisher Hannah Rahill
Executive Editor Sarah Putman Clegg
Editor Lauren Hancock

VP and Creative Director Gaye Allen
Associate Creative Director Emma Boys
Art Director Marisa Kwek
Senior Designer Renée Myers

Production Director Chris Hemesath
Production Manager Michelle Duggan
Color Manager Teri Bell

ACKNOWLEDGEMENTS
Weldon Owen would like to thank the following individuals
for their kind assistance in making this book a reality:

Photographer Kana Okada
Food Stylist Karen Shinto
Prop Stylist Lauren Hunter
Photographer's Assistants Angelica Cao and Paul Hammond
Food Stylist's Assistant Jeffrey L. Larsen

Copy Editor Sharron Wood
Consulting Editor Carolyn Miller
Proofreaders Desne Ahlers and Carolyn Keating
Indexer Ken DellaPenta

Special thanks to Jennifer Newens, Dawn Yanagihara, and Donita Boles
for their gracious assistance with the photography.
Additional photography by Ray Kachatorian, page 105; Dan Goldberg,
pages 148 and 172; Shutterstock, page 173.
Charity Ferreira extends special thanks to Sarah Epstein
and Marlene Kawahata.